He Freed Britain's Slaves

HE FREED BRITAIN'S SLAVES

Charles Ludwig

HERALD PRESS
Scottdale, Pennsylvania
Kitchener, Ontario
1977

Library of Congress Cataloging in Publication Data
Ludwig, Charles, 1918-
　He freed Britain's slaves.

　Bibliography: p.
　1. Wilberforce, William, 1759-1833.　2. Abolitionists. I. Title.
HT1029.W5L8　　326'.092'4 [B]　　77-9521
ISBN 0-8361-1822-7

HE FREED BRITAIN'S SLAVES
Copyright © 1977 by Herald Press, Scottdale, Pa. 15683
　Published simultaneously in Canada by Herald Press,
　Kitchener, Ont. N2G 4M5
Library of Congress Catalog Card Number: 77-9521
International Standard Book Number: 0-8361-1822-7
Printed in the United States of America
Design: Alice B. Shetler

10 9 8 7 6 5 4 3 2 1

To the memory of the slave, Quamina.
He qualified as a night watchman, but
due to bad legs was valued at only sixpence.

CONTENTS

Author's Preface 9

1. Captain Beef 19
2. Twisting Currents 28
3. William Wilberforce, M.P. 42
4. Boredom 52
5. The Zong 61
6. Conversion 76
7. Crusade 87
8. Dimensions of Hell 97
9. Calico Guts 110
10. Painful Compromise 120
11. A New Demosthenes 130
12. Defeat 140
13. Defeated Again 150
14. Delaying Tactics 160
15. Discouragement 167
16. Victory at Last 175
17. A New Dawn 191

Bibliography 205
The Author 208

AUTHOR'S PREFACE

The first Englishman to transport slaves from Africa to the New World was Sir John Hawkins. This was in 1562—a mere seventy years after Columbus had discovered the West Indies. Queen Elizabeth was shocked. She declared the affair was "detestable and would call down the vengeance of heaven."

But the Queen's reaction didn't frighten sharp-bearded Hawkins. He responded by lugging his account books to the palace. Entranced by the sight of such a pile of "easy" money, Good Queen Bess decided the business wasn't detestable after all. Indeed, she became so excited she lent Sir John a ship in which to transport slaves. This ship was the 700-ton *Jesus of Lubeck,* which had been purchased by Elizabeth's father, Henry VIII, for the English navy.

The heavily armed *Jesus*—now a slaver—was the largest British ship to enter the Caribbean during the sixteenth century. According to estimates, it was twice as large as the *Nina, Pinta,* and *Santa María* combined. Its main use to Hawkins, however, was not its size—rather it was that it gave unofficial approval to his new business. This approval soothed his conscience for, after all, Queen Elizabeth was the head of the Church of England!

By 1564 the swashbuckling Hawkins had four slavers. As these ships heaved at anchor while being readied for Africa, Sir John piously summoned his crews and issued orders which have become a tradition in the British Navy. "Serve God daily, love one another, preserve your victuals, beware of fire, and keep good company," he said.

The *Trade*, as the transportation of slaves to the New World was popularly known, was not new. A license to ship slaves had been issued by Charles V forty-five years before. As emperor of the Holy Roman Empire, Charles believed Negro slaves were a necessity if the newly discovered lands were to be developed. This was because American Indians usually died when forced into slavery.

Since the *1493 Line of Demarcation* bull issued by Pope Alexander VI barred Spain from Africa, Spain issued *asientos* to other nations to supply slaves for her colonies. This license was a valued possession. In 1600 it belonged to Portugal, forty years later it was transferred to the Dutch, and in 1701 it was given to France.

At the end of the War of Spanish Succession, the asiento was transferred from France to Britain as part of the Treaty of Utrecht in 1713. The agreement authorized Britain to supply the Spanish colonies with 4,800 slaves annually for a certain length of time. This treaty expired in 1739 and Philip V refused to reissue it. Incensed, Britain sought a quarrel with Spain in order to renew the contract and gather other advantages. The excuse came when Robert Jenkins claimed a Spaniard had cut off his ear. (Yes, it was even bottled and exhibited to Parliament!) The War of Jenkins' Ear which followed produced a new asiento and England became the world's largest slave trader. An English authority estimated that between 1680 and 1786 Britain transported "over two million slaves" to the New World.*

Ironically, as the British swung their swords and fired their cannon, they did so while singing James Thomson's stirring new hymn:

> Rule, Britannia, Britannia, rule the waves:
> Britons never, never, never will be slaves.

Apparently the stouthearted Britons considered being slaves and making slaves entirely different matters!

Because the Trade produced a lot of money, successful captains became an arrogant lot. They could be seen swinging down the streets sporting silver and even gold buttons, shoe buckles made of precious metals, and accompanied by a black slave dressed in the latest fashion.

The Trade lined the pockets and national treasuries of many European countries. Across the years the profit motive improved the system until not a move was wasted. And since some of the "Christian" nations were uneasy about what was being done, the Middle Passage was developed.

This new system was extremely simple. When slavers sailed from Bristol or Liverpool for Africa, they were loaded with merchandise: guns, beads, cloth, iron bars, brandy. These items were then retailed in Africa or traded for slaves.

After the ships were emptied of merchandise, they were loaded with slaves and sent directly to the Sugar Is-

---

* In turn, the Spanish denounced the English as "heretical dogs" and declared than an English captain had forced a Spanish nobleman to cut off his own nose and then eat it! Horace Walpole insisted that Jenkins died with both ears intact.

lands—the West Indies. Here, the slaves were sold and the ships were filled with West Indian products: rum, spices, molasses, and especially sugar. Finally, these valuables were unloaded in the same English ports from which they had sailed. Thus, the Englishman on the street was almost, but not quite, unaware of what was taking place in the distant section of the triangular voyage. And those who did know were tight-lipped because of the money their shares were earning in the business.

In the early days, the entire western bulge of Africa from the Senegal River in the north to Cape Lopez, just south of the equator, was known as Guinea. At first, the slavers cruised up and down the coast looking for smoke signals which indicated that there were slaves for sale. Soon, however, this system was improved by the establishment of "factories"—gathering places for the slaves.

Generally the slaves who lingered in the factories waiting to be sold were obtained from the interior. Slavers had developed many ways to capture victims. One was to create wars between neighboring villages and then to buy the captured warriors and their families from the victors. Another extremely productive method was devised by the chiefs themselves. Thirsting for the white man's brandy, a chief would accuse one of his subjects of witchcraft or some other crime and force him to take a test. A popular test was to force the accused to drink poisoned water. If the man vomited he was considered guilty and was sold to an eager trader for a few bottles of brandy.

Having purchased the slaves, the captain of the ship then had them branded—generally with a silver branding iron. (The silver irons caused less infection.)

Some tribes were considered more valuable than others. Coromantes, for example, were deemed to be too wild to make good slaves. To discourage their purchase, it was suggested that a special sales tax of ten pounds be levied on each . However, one captain recalled that Ibo children screamed with pain when they were branded, while the Coromantes went through the ordeal without wincing.

Slaves were usually packed into the ships at night to lessen their fears about what was going to happen to them. Most had never seen the ocean until they reached the factory, and the majority of them felt certain that they were destined to be eaten.

The method of packing the slaves divided the captains into two groups: the "loose packers" and the "tight packers." The loose packers argued that by giving the slaves more room and better food, fewer died en route, and thus the shareholders made more money. The others countered that although more died when they were tightly packed, the profits soared because more slaves were delivered.

During a period when the Trade was being investigated by Parliament, experts were sent to measure the 320-ton *Brookes*. This ship had carried as many as 609 slaves on one voyage. Like others, the captain possessed a chart which enabled him to cram the ship to the utmost. His chart allotted a space sixteen inches wide and six feet long for each male—and less for women. Since every inch was worth money to the owners, the children were coffined into even tighter quarters.

Most slavers arranged for their slaves to lie on their right sides "to protect their hearts." The slaves were shackled in pairs. Leg-irons bound the right ankle of one to the left ankle of another and handcuffs bound the right wrist of one to the left wrist of the other.

The floor of the hold was thus a solid mass of human beings wedged together like spoons in a drawer. But this was just the beginning, for generally there was a wide shelf directly overhead. This second floor, from two and a half to three feet above was also sardined with slaves.

Buckets were provided for the necessities of nature, but since the slaves were chained two by two, it was often difficult for the one to persuade the other to go with him. This was especially true when members of rival tribes were locked together. Because of this there were many "accidents" and quite often victims had to lie in their own filth or another's for hours or even days.

At the time, many Europeans felt that night air was dangerous to the health, and so the portholes were frequently closed. At times there was so little oxygen in the holds it was difficult to keep a candle burning. In addition to these problems the slaves were not used to the sea and most of them became sick. As a result of this inhuman treatment, the stench of a slaver could be detected as many as five miles away.

In good weather the slaves were required to go to the top deck where they were forced to jump up and down in their shackles. During such exercises crude rhythmic music was played. Often a captain advertised for "a person who can play the bagpipes for a Guinea ship."

Any slave who refused to jump was encouraged to do so with a cat-o'-nine-tails. Frequently the slaves jumped until their legs were raw and the irons crimson.

While the slaves jumped, their holds were swabbed with buckets of vinegar in which red-hot bullets had been dropped. The sailors hated the job and often refused with the result that many a sailor was himself flogged to death.

As a result of such harsh treatment a high percentage of both slaves and sailors perished during the Middle Passage. Many who knew the grim facts of the Trade were horrified. Popes, artists, Protestant bishops, Quakers, and journalists lashed out at the cruelties. But even though they described the sharks who feasted by following the ships across the Atlantic, they were helpless to put a stop to the system. There were too many lords and others in high places who profited from it.

At a time when those who hated every aspect of slavery feared that theirs was a lost cause, William Wilberforce, a tiny shrimp of a man, appeared on the scene.

Barely five feet tall, Wilberforce was so nearsighted he twisted his head to one side and thus appeared to be slightly hunched. He was plagued by illness most of his life. In desperation one of his doctors once declared that he had "calico guts" and could not live. Two things, however, he did not lack—courage and faith in God.

A reporter who visited the House of Commons remembered: "Another little man, as thin as a shadow, and drawing one side of his body after him, as if paralytic, hurried across the floor with a tottering brisk step, and awkward bow, and said in substance, that schools in Ireland were more desirable, and should be organized by all means. These few words were extremely well spoken, with peculiar energy of feeling, and in a manner graceful and impressive. This was Mr. Wilberforce. Nothing can surpass the meanness of his appearance, and he seems half blind."

When Wilberforce started to fight slavery, he felt like

an ant trying to crush an elephant. But his cause was one in which he believed and so he never gave up. It took a lifetime to accomplish his purpose. At times it seemed destiny was against him. His faith, however, never wavered, and his purpose was eventually accomplished. Today his body rests in Westminster Abbey, and those who know the story of his life speak of him in hallowed tones.

Charles Ludwig
Tucson, Arizona

He Freed Britain's Slaves

1
CAPTAIN BEEF

"MASTER WILBERFORCE, that was a most impertinent question!" exploded John Beef, his enormous cauliflower nose flaring like a pair of trombones.

The weather-beaten man, owner and captain of a 300-ton slaver, swiveled his good eye around the table. Churning with anger, it rested on each of the dozen guests. Then it paused accusingly on William Wilberforce, crouched at his right elbow like an undecided squirrel. As his stare attempted to pin the smartly dressed youth to the paneled wall, the captain's enormous right hand automatically opened the lid of an ivory snuffbox. With two thick fingers and a thumb, he greedily scooped up a large supply of snuff.

Holding the vile tobacco in midair, his eye continued to spurt fire at Wilberforce. He put the snuff to his nose, changed his mind, and then with the load still halfway to that prowlike appendage, remarked, "I've been sailin' the seas for more'n thirty years, and this is the first time I've been asked such an impertinent question." His eye stabbed at each guest again. In new fury, it rested on Wilberforce. "Would you care to repeat that question?" he challenged, his good eye bulging.

As the stares of the guests combined with those of the captain, Wilberforce leaned forward. Unconsciously his well-shaped head bent slightly to one side.

"Yes, I will repeat my question," he replied coolly. He spoke in a smooth, musical voice. "My question is, Doesn't it hurt your Christian conscience to buy and sell slaves—especially when you know that many of them are doomed to die in the Middle Passage?"

"No, it don't," said Beef, lifting his hands and shrugging. "Don't the Good Book say that we should go into all the world?"

"That's what it says," agreed Wilberforce. "But it says to go into all the world and preach the gospel. Are you proclaiming good news—and that is what the gospel is—when you jam your ship so full of slaves they're like books on a shelf?"

"Indeed I am. And that's the reason my ship is called the *John the Baptist.* By takin' slaves to the Sugar Islands I'm giv'n 'em a chance to become civilized Christians. In a way, I'm a missionary! Now there ain't no harm in that." He rolled his eye toward heaven and clasped his jeweled hands together as if in prayer.

"The Bible says the gospel is for 'whosoever will,' " Wilberforce said. "Do these blacks that you buy for a few bars of iron or a cheap gun or two want to go with you? Captain Beef, this is 1773 and here in England we believe in human dignity and freedom! Have you forgotten Magna Charta?"

"I'll admit that the guests on my ship are involuntary," Beef retorted. "I'll even admit that some of them die during the crossing. Still, I'm a-doin' 'em a lot of good. You should hear them sing!" He paused long enough to load each nostril with a loud sniff followed by a low *ahhh* as the powdered tobacco was drawn into place. "Slaving has some bad features," he continued. "We all know that. Still, every nation has practiced it. Slavery is even approved in the Bible."

A shaft of sunlight broke through a yellow pane in one of the castle's nearby windows. By this light, for the first time, Wilberforce noticed that a black youth, approximately his own age, was sitting on a high stool directly behind the captain. The slave was dressed in a flashy blue coat trimmed with gold braid and loaded with brass buttons. His kinky hair was high and neatly combed.

"I understand that you brand all of your victims," said Wilberforce. "Is that true, and is it necessary?"

"I resent your calling them my victims," replied the captain, glaring again. "The blacks on my ship are not my victims. They are my involuntary guests. And yes, I do brand them. But I brand them with a silver branding iron to minimize infection. And what's wrong with that? The blacks like to decorate their faces. They pay a witch doctor a rooster and sometimes even a goat to cut all sorts of fancy patterns into their skins. And I do it for free! Yes, sir, I do it for free. I don't even charge a farthing. And my brand is a fancy one. It says 'JB.' "

Beef jerked a thumb toward his slave. "This is Socrates," he said grandly. "I brought him and his mother over from Guinea seven years ago. You should have seen his ma. She had tribal scars all over her face. Unfortunately, she died at sea. Because of her death, I decided to keep Socrates. He can speak English almost as well as any of you. Besides, he can read and write. If it hadn't been for me he'd be sleeping in a mud hut paved with cow dung and filled with chickens and goats. Isn't that so, Socrates?"

"Yes, Captain Beef, that is so," replied Socrates, flashing a fine set of white teeth.

"And I feed you well. Isn't that so, Socrates?"

"Yes Captain Beef, that is so."

"And you wouldn't want to go back to Africa, would you?"

"No, I wouldn't, Captain Beef."

"Well, there you have it," said Beef. "Now, as some of you know my ship is in the docks at Bristol, and I need to raise some more money for my next voyage to Africa. If you'll contact me, I'll give you an idea about how much interest you can make if you care to invest in my enterprise."

Suddenly Lord Dawson stepped into the room. "It's time for cards," he said. "Follow me. Supper will be ready at six."

As the guests were moving into the next room, Wilerforce said to the slaver, "Do you mind if I stay and visit with Socrates?"

Beef glowered at him. "You know, Wilberforce, you not only look like a shrimp. You talk like a shrimp, you act like a shrimp, and you think like a shrimp. If it hadn't been that I sailed with your father in the Baltic, I wouldn't have answered a single one of those nasty questions."

Changing the subject, Wilberforce said, "Captain Beef, I know you've traveled a lot, and know a lot of things I'll never know. What do you think of this tea bill that was passed by Parliament last May?"

Beef looked startled. "You sure can change from one subject to another quicker'n anyone I've ever knowed." He rubbed his lowest chin and adjusted the band holding the patch over his left eye, "Tell you what I think. I think it's just and reasonable."

"Will the colonies accept it?"

"That, I doubt. They made such a howl in '65 over the Stamp Act, Parliament reversed itself. That was a big mistake. Parliament, says I, should never knuckle to the mob. But say, boy, you ain't old enough to be a-thinkin' about what goes on in Parliament! How old are you?"

"Fourteen."

"Hmm. That's 'bout the same age as Socrates. Of course no one knows how old he is. His ma didn't even know. Bought him and the woman for three bottles of rum. That wrinkled old chief was sure thirsty!" He started to leave. Then he remembered the snuffbox. "Can't get along without that," he mumbled, shoving it into his coat pocket. "A pinch now and then is as necessary as a hymnbook is to a screechin' Methodist."

"I hate cards," said Wilberforce. "Mind if I stay and talk to Socrates?"

Beef hesitated. He clawed at his cheek and polished the heavy gold buttons on his coat. "Solid gold!" he muttered, swiveling his eye. "Had 'em made out of gold from Guinea. Got the stuff from the same mines the Duke of York got his in the days of Charles II. The crafty duke used it to make the first guinea, so named to advertise his slavin' business. In them good old days a guinea was worth up to forty shillings instead o' the miserable twenty-one as now. That's why I had me buttons beat out o' Guinea gold. Only the best is good enough for a slave captain, says I."

"But what about my question?" persisted Wilberforce.

Beef snorted and his eye flamed again. "You never give up, do you? If you was on the *John the Baptist,* I'd have you in irons! Don't you know that rich people don't talk to slaves. I—" His voice trailed in contempt.

"Please."

"Oh, all right. But don't arrange for him to be baptized!" The captain followed this admonition with an oath and then strode out of the room with the grand rolling walk of an admiral in His Majesty's navy.

"You are a brave boy," said Socrates, shaking his head. "I've seen Captain Beef hang sailors to the yardarm for saying less than you said! It was all I could do to keep from cheering."

"Isn't he good to you?"

"Oh, he feeds me tolerably well and dresses me in the latest style. But that's to make him look better. You see I'm a symbol of his wealth. That's why he named me Socrates."

"Isn't that your real name?"

"Of course not! Since you live in Hull, on the east coast, you don't see much of slavery. But if you lived on the west coast, especially in Liverpool or Bristol, you'd know more about it.

"Lots of slave captains come to Beef's house," Socrates continued. "And most of them have a slave boy to wait on them. You should hear their fancy names!" He rolled his eyes and looked toward the ceiling. "Captain Jacks has one named Scipio, and Captain Crump named his Julius Caesar!"

Suddenly Wilberforce noticed the wide silver collar around Socrates' neck. "And what's this?" he asked, smoothing it with his finger.

"That's to keep me from running way! Notice what it says on the side by the lock." Socrates hunched down and Wilberforce read: "Captain John Beef, Negro Row—Liverpool."

"I never in my life saw such a thing!" exclaimed Wilberforce. He squinted at it again and rubbed his eyes.

"That's because you have a white skin and live in another world. There's a shop in Liverpool that advertises: *'Collars for Dogs & Blacks.'* I've seen it with my own eyes. Beef is really proud of that collar. Makes me polish it as if it were a crown jewel."

Changing his mood, Socrates asked, "Do you know Sam Johnson?"

"You mean Dictionary Johnson?"

"That's right. I know his servant, Francis Barber. Barber used to be a slave, but when his master, Colonel Bathurst, died, he was given his freedom. Dr. Johnson loves him like a son. He even pays him wages. Well, Barber got me interested in reading. Captain Beef doesn't like it very well, but I've even read a wee bit of Shakespeare."

"William! We need you in a card game," called Mrs. Wilberforce from the doorway.

"I'll be there in a minute," he replied.

"Hurry, we're waiting." She closed the door.

"Please, Socrates, tell me why Captain Beef doesn't want you to be baptized."

"That's a long story," replied Socrates, his handsome brown face turning a shade darker. "If he learned I'd been baptized his teeth would rattle."

"Why?"

"Because when a person is baptized—that is baptized into the Established Church—he receives a godfather, and—"

"William Wilberforce, come this very moment!" his mother demanded from the doorway.

"Yes, Mama, I'm coming," he said, rising to his feet.

Just before he left, Socrates slipped a small package into his hand. "Hide it in your coat, and don't let anyone see it," he whispered in a tone of desperation.

"William, you shouldn't spend your time talking to your inferiors—especially slaves!" his mother scolded. "And now you'd better brush your hair. Lord Dawson and the others want you to sing and do an imitation."

Peering at a full-length mirror, Wilberforce studied himself critically. He was only about four and a half feet tall, thin as a musket, with his head twisted to one side. He agreed that he did look like a shrimp, just as the captain had said. With vigorous strokes, he brushed his light brown hair. It had been cut across the top of his forehead, and the sides extended to the center of his ears.

He adjusted his lace collar and removed some hairs from his knee-length breeches. After running a cloth over his silver shoe buckles and making certain that his full-length stockings were taut and straight, he stepped with confidence into the card room.

Following cards, the guests were shooed into the spacious, candlelit dining room, where they faced an enormous table loaded with Wedgewood—the rage of the day.

This was the seventh time that month he had been forced to endure such a feast and he felt like an overstuffed python. The sight and smell—and even the clink of the dishes—turned his stomach. The first course included a large cod with staring eyes, an enormous section of mutton with ribs sticking up from the backbone like posts in an old fence, a thick soup, chicken pie, and dark pudding, and rolling hills of potatoes, carrots, and onions.

The second course consisted of roast pigeon, fillet of veal smothered with mushrooms and a hot sauce, asparagus, baked sweetbreads, lobster, apricot tart, and a pyramid of syllabubs with various jellies at the base. He started to complain, but his mother's stare stopped him. For dessert, there were heaping baskets of fruit, followed by a variety of wines.

When no one could possibly down another mouthful, a guest said, "Now, William, we must have an imitation." Wilberforce was ready. With precise tones and gestures he mimicked David Garrick's rendition of Hamlet's soliloquy. With deep feeling, he worked through the lines "To be, or not to be."

"You should appear on the stage," applauded Lady Dawson.

"Not on the stage. You should be in Parliament!" exclaimed another.

"Oh, no. Not in Parliament," objected Captain Beef, shaking his chins. "If he ever got to Parliament he'd free the slaves!"

"And that I would," agreed Wilberforce.

2
TWISTING CURRENTS

IT WAS ONE O'CLOCK in the morning when Wilberforce stepped through the door of his room to prepare for bed. The routine social events which his mother forced him to endure two and three times a week had become a bore. He stifled a yawn and then stirred up the nearly dead coals in the fireplace. It was late October and cold winds were already coming in from the North Sea.

Before kneeling at his bedside—a habit he had learned from his Methodist uncle and aunt—he read a few verses from the New Testament. Then he slipped between the cool sheets. Normally he was a good sleeper. But tonight the scenes of the day kept coming before him. All at once he remembered the package Socrates had given him.

He tried to ignore his curiosity about what might be in the package. But he kept remembering the desperate tones in Socrates' voice. Finally he gave up. Creeping softly out of bed so as not to awaken his mother, he lit a candle in the fireplace and placed it in a silver stand on his desk. Next, he fumbled through his pockets until he located the package.

Slightly larger than his hand, the parcel was wrapped in heavy parchment and tied with a thick, black thread. He was trying to unknot the thread when his door opened.

"I see you're still up," said his mother, entering the room. She carried a candle in one hand and a sheaf of papers in the other. A nightcap was pulled tight over her head. Quickly Wilberforce slipped the package between a row of books on his shelf.

"Lady Dawson gave me a wonderful recipe today," she shrilled. "I'm so excited, I must share it with you. It's exactly what we need for a Christmas party. I'm already making a list of guests." William had returned to bed and so she pulled up a chair. "Just listen," she said eagerly.

"Mine will be the biggest minced pie ever baked in Hull! Here's what we'll need. Two rabbits, a pheasant, a capon, two pigeons, and a hare. After these have been cooked—Let's see." She held the recipe closer to the candle. "Yes, the recipe says: 'The meat from these should be separated from the bones and chopped into a fine hash. Then add the following: the hearts and livers from all of these animals along with two sheep kidneys.' " She paused to emphasize this vital information and then went on.

" 'After the above has been prepared, stir in a supply

of meatballs mixed with eggs. And now the spices. Add pickled mushrooms, salt, pepper, vinegar—and a generous supply of other spices which you might have, especially those from the land of our blessed Lord. This done, carefully pour everything into a crust of pastry and bake it until well done.'

"Now what do you think of that?"

"Sounds pretty filling," William said. "Do you think the cook could do all that by himself?"

"Not by himself, but maybe the gardener and the butler could help. Henry and Clarence are always ready to help in a pinch. I'm sure we could manage. Doesn't it sound delicious?"

"I think it would taste better if we added one more thing," said William, sitting up.

"And what could that be?"

"John Beef! But you'd have to cut off his buttons first. I'd hate to choke on one."

"Oh, come now, William. Let's be serious!"

"Mama, as I listened to that slaver and noticed how calloused everyone was when he spoke about his 'involuntary guests,' it made me sick. It was all I could do to eat. Mama, were any of my relatives slavers?"

"None. The Wilberforces were in the shipping business for just around a century. But no one, as far as I know, ever traded in slaves. Most of our trade was in the Baltic. I can still hear your father talking about the timber he bought in Sweden; the hemp, flax, and iron from Norway, Prussia, and even Russia. Your father, William, was a very honest and great man."

"I'm relieved to hear that. Mama, I just can't get those slaves out of my mind. Did you see Socrates with that collar around his neck?"

He tried to ignore his curiosity about what might be in the package. But he kept remembering the desperate tones in Socrates' voice. Finally he gave up. Creeping softly out of bed so as not to awaken his mother, he lit a candle in the fireplace and placed it in a silver stand on his desk. Next, he fumbled through his pockets until he located the package.

Slightly larger than his hand, the parcel was wrapped in heavy parchment and tied with a thick, black thread. He was trying to unknot the thread when his door opened.

"I see you're still up," said his mother, entering the room. She carried a candle in one hand and a sheaf of papers in the other. A nightcap was pulled tight over her head. Quickly Wilberforce slipped the package between a row of books on his shelf.

"Lady Dawson gave me a wonderful recipe today," she shrilled. "I'm so excited, I must share it with you. It's exactly what we need for a Christmas party. I'm already making a list of guests." William had returned to bed and so she pulled up a chair. "Just listen," she said eagerly.

"Mine will be the biggest minced pie ever baked in Hull! Here's what we'll need. Two rabbits, a pheasant, a capon, two pigeons, and a hare. After these have been cooked—Let's see." She held the recipe closer to the candle. "Yes, the recipe says: 'The meat from these should be separated from the bones and chopped into a fine hash. Then add the following: the hearts and livers from all of these animals along with two sheep kidneys.'" She paused to emphasize this vital information and then went on.

"'After the above has been prepared, stir in a supply

of meatballs mixed with eggs. And now the spices. Add pickled mushrooms, salt, pepper, vinegar—and a generous supply of other spices which you might have, especially those from the land of our blessed Lord. This done, carefully pour everything into a crust of pastry and bake it until well done.'

"Now what do you think of that?"

"Sounds pretty filling," William said. "Do you think the cook could do all that by himself?"

"Not by himself, but maybe the gardener and the butler could help. Henry and Clarence are always ready to help in a pinch. I'm sure we could manage. Doesn't it sound delicious?"

"I think it would taste better if we added one more thing," said William, sitting up.

"And what could that be?"

"John Beef! But you'd have to cut off his buttons first. I'd hate to choke on one."

"Oh, come now, William. Let's be serious!"

"Mama, as I listened to that slaver and noticed how calloused everyone was when he spoke about his 'involuntary guests,' it made me sick. It was all I could do to eat. Mama, were any of my relatives slavers?"

"None. The Wilberforces were in the shipping business for just around a century. But no one, as far as I know, ever traded in slaves. Most of our trade was in the Baltic. I can still hear your father talking about the timber he bought in Sweden; the hemp, flax, and iron from Norway, Prussia, and even Russia. Your father, William, was a very honest and great man."

"I'm relieved to hear that. Mama, I just can't get those slaves out of my mind. Did you see Socrates with that collar around his neck?"

"Yes, I saw him. He was dressed like a prince. Don't you agree with the captain that he's better off as a slave than he was in all that dreadful filth in Africa?"

"Never! That collar with its lock looks like a dog's collar. Socrates is a boy, not a bulldog! Mama, no one has the right to own another human being. All of us are equal in the sight of God."

"Perhaps you are right, William." She stifled a yawn. "But don't get too concerned about it. You could ruin your health—which isn't very good as it is. You're fortunate just to be alive. I still remember when you were born. It was on August 24—a scorching St. Bartholomew's Day—in 1759. Seems like yesterday. And as I've told you before, you were born in this very house!

"Friends said that you'd be unlucky because St. Bartholomew's Day is connected with that frightful massacre of the Huguenots in Paris. But I don't believe such rubbish. The thing that worried your father and me was that you were such a wee bit of a thing. You weren't any bigger than a pair of lobsters! If you'd been born in Roman times, they'd have thrown you out to die."

"But, Mama, we can't ignore slavery because it's upsetting. How'd you like to be captured, branded, crammed into a filthy ship and made to work day and night without wages? If slavery is wrong, we must end it."

Glancing at the clock, Mrs. Wilberforce exclaimed, "Dear me, it's already two-thirty. Let's get some rest. I'll have a long mother-to-son talk with you in the morning after breakfast."

After the light in his mother's room had been out for half an hour, Wilberforce lit a candle and picked up the packet. As he worked at the knot, he kept his ears alert for the sound of steps.

The packet was filled with newspaper clippings—and a drawing. All of the clippings except one were small advertisements. The exception was a long article with a bold headline. The half-inch heading said: *ABOLITIONISTS THOMAS CLARKSON AND GRANVILLE SHARP AT IT AGAIN!*

Wilberforce was only vaguely aware of the meaning of the word *abolitionist* and so he put the article to one side and spread the advertisements on his bed. One, so worn he could barely read it, had been in *The London Advertiser* in 1756. It read:

> To be sold, a Negro Boy, about fourteen years old, warranted free from any distemper, and has had those fatal to that color; has been used two years to all kinds of housework, and to wait at table; his price is £25, and would not be sold but the person he belongs to is leaving off business. Apply at the bar of the George Coffee-house, in Chancery Lane, over against the Gate.

A better preserved clipping was from *The Public Advertiser* of November 28, 1769. Holding it close to his eyes, Wilberforce read:

> To be sold, a Black Girl, the property of J.B.; eleven years of age, who is extremely handy, works at her needle tolerably, and speaks English perfectly well; is of excellent temper and willing disposition. Inquire of Mrs. Owen, at the Angel Hotel, behind St. Clement's Church in the Strand.

The drawing was that of the slaver, *Jesus of Lubeck*. The detail was excellent. It showed the top-heavy decks, the four masts, the crow's nest, and even the curved sickles at the end of the yardarms. These murderous sickles, Wilberforce knew, had been attached so that in close combat with another ship, the *Jesus* could slash the ropes of the enemy.

Added to this historic picture—Wilberforce had seen similer ones before—was a stream of slaves being thrown overboard and the fin of a shark awaiting its meal. The drawing, he decided, was nearly as good as a sketch by Hogarth, it was signed: Socrates.

Carefully, he replaced the items in the packet, and then hid it at the end of a drawer. He blew out the candle and tried to go to sleep. But now he was even more awake than before.

The face of Socrates, along with the collar, came before him. He kept wondering what would develop if the lad could go to art school. Next he remembered Captain John Beef. His nose seemed larger than ever. And then it seemed that he could hear him speaking again. "Don't arrange for him to be baptized."

Half-awake, Wilberforce wondered why Beef didn't want him to be baptized. After all, he had compared his trade to that of a missionary. There must be some reason. . . . Still wondering about this, he fell asleep.

As he dozed, he dreamed that he was a bishop. Just as he reached into the font for water to sprinkle Socrates, an iron hand stopped him.

Sometime later—he didn't know how long—he dreamed that he was in Africa and was being branded. A full-bearded white man with enormous teeth held him on the ground with a knee in his stomach while an aide pressed a white-hot branding iron into his shoulder. As he squirmed, he could feel the heat and smell the smoke. Then he was awakened by the sound of banging kettles.

He opened his eyes to discover that the morning sun had provided the heat in his nightmare, and that the smell of his burning flesh was really only the smell of toast being prepared in the fireplace.

He had overslept.

"William, I was proud of you last night," began Elizabeth Wilberforce, his mother. "You have a marvelous voice, your diction is perfect, and you are a great actor. Several ladies told me that someday you will represent Hull in Parliament!

"But, William. . . ." A frown crossed her face as she thoughtfully refilled her cup with tea. "I'm disappointed that you're still clinging to some of that horrid Methodist extremism you got from your uncle and aunt."

"What do you mean?"

"Well, you're reluctant to play cards—and you insisted on speaking to that slave boy. William, you must never forget that your father was one of Hull's leading merchants, and that your grandfather was a friend of the Duke of Marlborough. The Wilberforce line goes clear back to Saxon times. Of course, the name was Wilberfoss in those days. Your—"

"Mama, you have the Methodists all wrong. They—"

"Don't interrupt me! It's time you learned something about your ancestors. There have been mayors and scholars and all sorts of distinguished people in the family. This house is even distinguished." She swept her hands toward the paneled walls, the great fireplace, the magnificent staircase, the tapestries, the fine paintings. "When Sir John Lister was mayor of Hull, he entertained Charles I in this very house. That, William, is a distinction!"

"I'm proud of my heritage. But the Methodists are great people—even though they do get a little excited. George Whitefield—"

"Yes, George Whitefield," interjected Mrs. Wilberforce. "Everyone knows about him. People of quality call him Dr. Squintim. He's the one who started preaching in the fields. Think of it! Preaching in the fields like a common clown. I'd be ashamed to admit that I'd ever seen the man."

"What do you think of David Garrick?" asked William, his eyes low on the eggcup by his plate.

"He's the greatest Shakespearean actor of the century. And you did a marvelous job imitating him."

"Do you know what Garrick thinks of Whitefield?"

"I really have no idea."

"Well, Garrick said that he'd be willing to walk twenty miles to hear him, and that he'd give a hundred guineas if he could say 'Oh' like George Whitefield!"

"I still don't like him."

"Mama, I don't want to make you feel bad, but George Whitefield put something in my heart that will always remain. I went with my aunt to hear him at Tottenham Court Chapel four years ago. The place was so filled we could barely get in. Still, we managed to find a seat near the front row. Oh, you should have heard him! His eloquence was like thunder, and earthquakes, and the waves of the sea all mixed together. He made us laugh and he made us cry until our throats ached. And when he got eloquent those piercing eyes of his seemed to cross just a wee bit. That's why they call him Dr. Squintim.

"He seemed to be able to look right into my soul. Mama, George Whitefield convinced me of two things.

He convinced me that God has a special work for everyone—including me—and that God has a mysterious providence that guides and helps all who trust Him."

"Nevertheless, I don't like him. Indeed, I don't like any of the Methodists—including John and Charles Wesley!" All at once she grew thoughtful. "William, you were not quite nine when your father died. At the time, I was so broken up I made one of the biggest mistakes of my life. I sent you to live at St. James' Place with your father's brother, Uncle William. For one reason or another I didn't realize that his wife was a half sister to John Thornton—another of those dreadful preachers. And even worse, I didn't realize that they were great friends of George Whitefield."

She stopped to butter a slice of toast.

"When I discovered my mistake, I brought you home and sent you to school at Pocklington. It's been costing me between £300 and £400 a year to keep you there. But if Master Basket can squeeze all of this nonsense out of you, I'll be satisfied."

"Mama, I like Basket. He serves us wonderful teas, and he doesn't make us work. But he'll never pry out of me those things I learned from the Methodists and from Aunt and Uncle William Wilberforce. You see, Mama, I was converted!"

"Converted!" She spat out the word with utter contempt and her face soured. "You weren't converted. You were perverted! As everyone knows, all of us in this house are Christians. We pray every day. We go to church twice a week. I'm not against Christianity. I'm just against fanaticism." She paused to poke the fire. "There's one thing you ought to know, William, and that is that your grandfather hates—no—loathes Methodism.

A while back he said to me, 'If Billy turns Methodist he shall not have a sixpence of mine!' You'd better take that as a warning. And remember, he's rich."

The conversation might have continued, but at that moment William's sister Sarah stepped into the room.

Wilberforce was unloading his things at Pocklington when he discovered the package that had been given him by Socrates. The boredom of the many suppers and balls that had followed that eventful night had pushed it completely out of his mind. Again he spread the contents, this time on the table, and glanced at them. The clippings about Clarkson and Sharp were there, and once again he was struck by the word "abolitionist." He made a mental note to look it up. And then he remembered Beef's stern warning about baptism. He was puzzling about this when a friend poked his head through the door. "Did you hear about the Boston Tea Party?" asked the boy with the face of an owl.

"You mean the tea this afternoon with Master Basket? I've heard it's going to be a big one."

"No, no. Not that. Don't you remember when the Fat One sent all that tea to Boston and insisted on putting a tax on it?"

"Of course, I remember. I asked Captain Beef what he thought about it. But—but just who is the Fat One?"

"Lord North, silly! Since he's been Prime Minister he does everything King George wants him to do. Father says that if North doesn't watch his step Britain will lose her American Colonies."

"All right. I understand. Now maybe you can explain what the Boston Tea Party is all about."

"Well, when the ships full of tea anchored at Boston,

some of the agitators dressed up like Indians and tossed the tea—the London papers say 342 chests of it—into the bay. I can imagine the Fat One's pretty worried and that good old William Pitt is giving him a bad time in the House of Lords. Pitt has always defended the colonies and now that he's the Earl of Chatham and doesn't have to be elected, he's become a real thorn to the King. I hope someday to go to London and listen to him from the gallery."

"Listen, Sam," said Wilberforce, "you live in Liverpool and your father is an advocate. Maybe you could tell me something I've been longing to know."

"Speak, thy servant is listening."

"Why is it that owners of slaves don't want them baptized?"

"Oh, that's easy. Father was engaged in such a case just a fortnight ago. You see the slaves think that if they are baptized they are made free under English law. That, of course, is still a disputed point. But when they are baptized they choose godfathers and the godfathers fight for them like fighting cocks in court. If I owned a slave I wouldn't even let him look pious!"

"What do you think of slavery?"

"I really don't know. Sometimes I think the poor devils are better off as slaves. But then—" He shrugged and adjusted his glasses. "Living in Liverpool, I see—and smell—a lot. During the vacation I saw a boy about our age being auctioned down on Negro Row. It was pretty terrible.

"His ankle, where the shackle had been on his way over, was so raw I could nearly see the bone; and it was such a cold day he was shivering from the weather. You should have seen the way the buyers examined him!

They acted as if he were a horse. They poked their dirty fingers in his mouth, thumped him on the chest, looked at the whites of his eyes, made him jump up and down, and felt his muscles.

"When the bidding started, one man called him a bag of bones, and another said he reminded him of a scarecrow. He finally went for £14. The affair turned my stomach."

"One more question. What is an abolitionist?"

"They're people—mostly Quakers—who want to abolish slavery."

"Then I'm an abolitionist!"

After Sam was gone, Wilberforce locked his door, lit a candle, and began to study the newspaper clippings about Thomas Clarkson and Granville Sharp. The story was about a former slave by the name of Thomas Lewis. While living in Chelsea, Robert Stapylton, his former owner, discovered him. He then hired John Malony and Aaron Armstrong, waterfront characters, to help him. A darkly smudged section of the clipping related what happened. "They seized the person of Thomas Lewis, an African slave, in a dark night, and dragged him to a boat lying in the Thames; they then gagged him and tied him with a cord, and rowed him down to a ship, and put him on board to be sold as a slave in Jamaica."

Scanning the next column, Wilberforce learned that Granville Sharp had been alerted to the kidnapping. On July 4, 1770, he miraculously secured a writ of habeas corpus and forwarded it to Spithead. Good fortune was his. Contrary winds had delayed the ship at the Downs.

A sharp rap at the door interrupted Wilberforce. "You'd better get ready for the tea with Master Basket," said Jim. "I saw some of the tarts and pastry. *Mmmm!* It's going to be—"

"Listen, Jim, I want you to hear something," said Wilberforce earnestly. He pointed to a chair. After explaining the first part of the story, he read out loud the next part of the clipping.

"The vessel on which the African had been dragged had reached the Downs, and had actually gotten under way to the West Indies. In two or three hours she would have been out of sight, but precisely at this critical moment the writ was served. The officer who gave it to the captain saw the poor man chained to the mainmast, bathed in tears and casting a last mournful look on the land of freedom. The captain, on receiving the writ, was outraged, but knowing the serious consequences of resisting the law of the land, he gave up his prisoner, whom the officer carried safe, but now crying for joy, to the shore."

"Sharp was lucky that time," said Jim getting up. "When he rescued the two slaves from the *Havannah*, one of the men's feet were so swollen, Sharp had to take him to St. Bartholomew's Hospital. The surgeon amputated both his legs just below the knee. It was a pity."

Jim stopped at the door, his hand on the latch. "You'd better hurry up, Billy, if you want to get in on that tea," he said.

"I—I don't think I'll go," mumbled Wilberforce. "My insides are beginning to twist."

Wilberforce laid down and tried to push what he had read and heard out of his mind. But it was lodged there as securely as a nail in a piece of oak. After an hour or two of misery, he got up, went to his desk, and wrote a letter attacking slavery. It was a strong letter and his quill glided effortlessly across the page. After rereading it, he blotted it with fine sand, folded it into a square, and sealed it with a dab of sealing wax.

The next day he addressed it to the editor of the York newspaper and handed it to a classmate named Walmsley. "Be a good fellow and mail it for me," he said.

As Walmsley disappeared from the campus, Wilberforce felt better than he had felt for a long time.

3
WILLIAM WILBERFORCE, M. P.

IN OCTOBER, 1776— a scant three months after the American Colonies had declared freedom from Great Britain—William Wilberforce enrolled at St. John's College in Cambridge. He was seventeen years old at the time.

Changing from the village school at Pocklington to a great university was an upsetting experience. He remembered: "I was introduced on the very first night of my arrival to as licentious a set of men as can well be conceived. They drank hard, and their conversation was even worse than their lives. I lived amongst them for some time, though I never relished their society. . . . Often, indeed, I was horror-stricken at their conduct . . .

and after the first year I shook off, in a great measure, my connection with them."

Wilberforce, however, was popular. He had more money to spend than most. His grandfather had just passed away and left him a fortune under the guardianship of his mother. Thinking of him in those university days, T. Gisborne wrote: "There was no one at all like him for powers of entertainment. Always fond of repartee and discussion, he seemed entirely free from conceit and vanity. There was always a great Yorkshire pie in his room, and all were welcome to partake of it. My room and his were back to back, and often when I was raking out my fire at ten o'clock, I heard his melodious voice calling aloud to me to come and sit with him before I went to bed. It was a dangerous thing to do, for his amusing conversation was sure to keep me up so late that I was behind-hand the next morning."

Wilberforce was not a grind. Still, he studied more than most and did well on examinations. He loved the classics and liked to memorize poetry. Mathematics was his horror.

"If I had your wealth, I wouldn't study so hard," remarked Jim one day in the library. "You don't have to sweat to get what you want. Slow down. Be a human being. Have some fun."

"Jim," replied Wilberforce, his finger on the page of the book he was reading, "it isn't hard work when you're doing what you know God wants you to do. That's one of the things I learned from the Methodists. Whitefield toiled night and day, and so do the Wesleys. They follow their carefully laid-out plans. They have methods. Work, to them, is not unpleasant—it is pleasure."

"You should be a preacher!" scoffed Jim.

During his freshman year, while on his way to a lecture, Wilberforce was stopped by a friend. "I want to introduce you to another William," said he. "This is William Pitt, son of the Earl of Chatham."

"You—you mean the former Prime Minister?" asked Wilberforce, a little startled.

"I—I guess so," shrugged Pitt uncomfortably. He rearranged the fat law books under his arm. "Nice to have met you, Wilberforce. But I must really be on my way. I'm going to a lecture on Cicero and it begins in three minutes."

Wilberforce could not forget him. He was impressed with Pitt's tall, slender frame, his finely chisled face, immaculate coat, snowy shirt, and knee breeches. A mysterious feeling assured him that this young man was destined to be an important part of his life. Quietly he started to observe, to make mental notes.

He learned that Pitt was only four months his senior and that he was already completing his third year at Pembroke. He also learned that he was passionately interested in law—and politics.

Pitt finished the work on his degree that year. And because he was the son of a peer he was not required to take the final examinations. Likewise, his rank entitled him to an honorary M.A. Pitt remained in Cambridge, however, taking advanced courses in mathematics and the classics. He especially liked Thucydides, Shakespeare, and Milton. And when Adam Smith published *The Wealth of Nations* in 1776, he devoured it. The book converted him to the Free Trade doctrine. He also worked at his public speaking. "Have to keep up with the old man," he explained.

Chatham passed away in 1778. This meant Pitt had to

go to work. A rich uncle rented an office for him in Lincoln's Inn and he began to practice law. He was not quite nineteen.

When Wilberforce left Cambridge in the summer of 1780, he was forced to make a decision about his future. "You have plenty of money. Live it up!" urged some of his rich friends. Another alternative was to manage the family business—a chore that was currently being performed by his cousin, Abel Smith. None of this appealed to him.

"I'm going to stand for Parliament," he announced.

"But—but you're only twenty," objected his mother.

"Yes, I know the law. But I'll be twenty-one on the twenty-fourth of August. And if the King waits a bit to dissolve Parliament—"

"Lord Rockingham is a power and a very determined man. Can you overcome him and his interests?"

"Certainly. Anyway, I think he likes me."

"What about Sir George Savile? He has lots of friends—and experience."

"Mama, I'm going to win. Don't worry. God will help me."

"Then I'm with you, Billy. I'll do all I can to help."

Wilberforce planned a thorough campaign. He made speeches, wrote articles, published ads, and knocked on doors. As he approached the home of Johnny Bell, the butcher, he hesitated. Johnny barely had enough property to qualify as a voter. "Should I request his vote?" he asked of a worker.

"Of course!" replied the man. "Bell is a fine fellow and if they give you a rough time, he'll come to your rescue."

About 300 potential Hull voters lived in London near

the Thames River. Since that many voters represented at least a fourth of the electorate, Wilberforce went to London to win them over. He visited them, arranged large suppers—and solicited support.

Whenever possible, he spent time in the gallery of the House of Commons. The debates on the war with the American Colonies fascinated him. France had joined the conflict on the American side in 1778, and the British thrust into North Carolina wasn't going well. This frustration stoked the heat in the speeches. Denunciation and sarcasm, along with spine-chilling flights of oratory, dominated the sessions.

Lord North, the Prime Minister, was usually present when Wilberforce visited. Fredrick North was most unpopular in the House. He was fat, suffered from gout, was awkward in his movements, and frequently lost important papers (one misplaced document was found in the men's room), and because his tongue was too large for his mouth, his speech was difficult to understand.

Even worse than these defects was the fact that King George III had paid his debts. Due to this generosity, it was believed that North was merely a tool in His Majesty's clumsy fingers.

North often sat on his padded seat with his head down and his eyes closed. Indeed, some said they feared he would snore. While in this condition, a member of the House began to denounce him. He berated him one way and then another. He orated on his sins of omission and those of commission. Then, shaking a bony finger at him, he snarled, "Even now, in the midst of these perils, the noble lord is asleep!"

"No, I'm not," replied North calmly, his gray eyes still closed. "But I wish to God that I was."

"Do you mind if I join you?" asked a resonant voice in the shadows. Wilberforce whirled and squinted into the darkness. "William Pitt!" he exclaimed, grabbing his friend's hand in both of his. "What in the world brings you here?"

"I'm standing for Cambridge. Came to relax. Nothing stimulates me more than sharp debate. Rumor has it that Burke's going to speak." Pitt slapped Wilberforce on the shoulder. "Heard you're standing for Hull. Hope you make it. They need a good man. But how can you be elected when you're not yet twenty-one?"

"I'll be old enough in time. Don't worry."

Unexpectedly, Edmund Burke leaped to his feet. "Sir," he began in his usual dynamic manner. His voice brought the silence of the tomb to the House, for everyone knew this journalist from Dublin had something to say—and that he always said it well. Wilberforce and Pitt leaned forward, their mouths slightly ajar. And when a member from Cork shouted, "Hear! Hear!" in agreement, they nodded their heads. Both agreed with Burke that the American war was a mistake.

At 3:00 a.m. the two hopefuls faced one another across a spotless table at Windsor—a coffeehouse at Charing Cross. "Wilberforce," said Pitt briskly, "we're fortunate to be alive! True, thanks to the Fat One, we'll be losing the colonies. But England is growing. Along with Wales, we have a population of nearly nine million! That means that if we could place His Majesty's subjects end to end—" He closed his eyes and made a calculation. "Yes, that means that all of those noble people would make a line 8,523 miles long. Of course, to arrive at that figure, I'm assuming that the average Englishman is five feet tall. That many people put end to end would stretch one third of the way around the world. London alone has around a million, and if—"

"Come on, Pitt," laughed Wilberforce. "Everyone knows that you are a mathematical genius. What I want to know is, What are you going to do in Parliament?"

"Well, first of all I'm going to be appointed Chancellor of the Exchequer. Then after filling that post for a few months I expect to be Prime Minister!"

Their conversation was interrupted by the waiter.

After stirring his coffee, Wilberforce said, "I've heard that you were with your father when he made his last speech in the House of Lords in '78. Could you tell me about it?"

Pitt smiled grimly. "I remember that day very well. It was April 7. How could I forget it? Father had been ill for a long time. His cheeks were as shrunken as those of a toothless old woman, and his circulation was so bad we had to keep his legs wrapped in flannel. The flesh on his head had thinned until his wig was much too large.

"As he hobbled around on his crutches, all of us knew he wouldn't be with us long. We tried to keep him inside, and we managed quite well for a long time. And then he learned that because France and Spain were about to join the Americans, the Duke of Richmond was going to propose that we negotiate with the colonies. This was more than he could stand and he began to pace around like a chained lion.

"Father was against the whole war. He was really for the Americans, but the idea that we would give up because of France was just too much for him. He hated the Bourbons!

"That morning, he put on his finest velvet coat—the one he had worn as Prime Minister—and we started out.

Lord Mahon (his son-in-law) went with us. Father was so tired when he entered the building he had to rest for a time in the Lord Chancellor's room. Then we led him into the House. As we slowly made our way a number of peers rose to make room, for the place was jammed.

"The Duke of Richmond made his motion, and then Father started getting to his feet. It was a slow, slow process. I could almost feel the pains in his joints myself. Tottering a little, his eyes swept over the assembly like an old eagle searching for prey. As he began, his voice was so low many cupped their hands behind their ears. But I didn't miss a word.

"Thank God that I have been enabled to come here this day to perform my duty,' he began. 'I am old and infirm. I have one foot, more than one foot, in the grave. I have risen from my bed to stand up in the cause of my country, perhaps never to speak in this House again. . . .'

"He went on and on in this fashion. Sometimes he stumbled. Occasionally he lost the thread of his thought. But his old eloquence was there. His last words, Billy, are part of my inheritance. Straightening up the best he could, he said:

" 'My lords, I rejoice that the grave has not closed upon me—that I am still alive to lift my voice against the dismemberment of this ancient and most noble monarchy! Shall this great kingdom now fall before the House of Bourbon? If we must fall, let us fall like men!' "

Pitt's eyes became tense and shadows from the candles made figures on his flushed cheeks. "When Father took his seat, there was almost a sigh of relief. The Duke of Richmond made a reply. It was moderate and polite. But as Father listened, his blood seemed to churn within him. He was like a volcano about to erupt.

"Every eye in the House was on him. Then he struggled to his feet. He started to speak, but the words wouldn't come. Instead, he placed his hand over his heart. He swayed for a moment and then collapsed. We got him into a house on Downing Street. He was buried in the Abbey and he deserved it.

"Billy, if I could only speak like my father, I'd be happy!"

"You will if you get involved in a cause larger than yourself. That's what the Methodists taught—and I believe it." Wilberforce spoke with confidence.

"You're right," said Pitt. "And if I get into power there are a number of things that must be done. We need reform. We need to rid ourselves of corruption and these rotten boroughs. We need to—"

"What about abolishing slavery?" interrupted Wilberforce.

"Yes, and we need to abolish slavery—every vestige of it!" Pitt doubled his fist. "I hate slavery with every part of my body, mind, and soul. It's a disease that must be cured."

"Bravo!" said Wilberforce. "I think you've found the cause that will make you speak even better than your father—and when you do, I'll let you know."

"Let's shake hands on that," said Pitt.

The date of the election in Hull was set for September 11. This removed the problem of his age and gave Wilberforce the opportunity to use his twenty-first birthday to advantage. He roasted an ox, provided cool drinks, and invited potential voters to the feast. In the days that remained, Wilberforce and his friends worked night and day to win every possible vote. Finally the great day came and the people went to the polls.

In due time, the results were published. Wilberforce held the newspaper close as he read:

Lord Manners 673
David Hartley 453
William Wilberforce..................1,126

"I made it!" he exclaimed, thumping the paper on the table. "I'm a member of Parliament—an M.P.! And look, Mama, I got as many votes as Manners and Hartley put together. This is the happiest day in my life. Pitt and I are going to work together, and—"

A knock at the door interrupted him.

Johnny Bell faced him. "I've found the man who threw the stone at you, and I'll kill him tonight," said the butcher, his face florid and eager.

"Kill him?" shuddered Wilberforce. "Don't do that! I don't believe in violence. Many thanks for your support."

But his joy didn't last, for on September 16 he learned that Pitt had been soundly defeated. Indeed, he had received only 142 votes and was at the bottom of the poll. As Wilberforce read the results, a block of ice seemed to settle in his stomach.

Maybe he wouldn't be able to help the slaves after all!

4
BOREDOM

FEW HAVE BEEN as well equipped to serve in the Parliament as auburn-haired William Pitt. Almost before he could read, his father would stand him on a stump in the park. Then he would say, "William, those trees are members of the House of Commons. Convince them that they should vote for the motion."

William Pitt practiced speaking and became so accomplished he astonished everyone. When he was only seven, his father was made Earl of Chatham. Dismayed, William said, "I'm glad I'm not the oldest son because I want to speak in the House of Commons like Papa." Even then he knew titles are inherited by the oldest son, and entitled persons to sit in the House of Lords.

Thus, although soundly defeated, Pitt knew exactly what to do—and when. He approached the Duke of Rutland. In turn, the Duke persuaded Sir James Lowther to help. Sir James controlled nine "pocket boroughs." Such districts were almost completely owned by one person or one family. Because of this, the owner could demand that his tenants or employees vote for his candidate. Pitt loathed the system. But anxious to enter the House, he forgot his conscience and accepted the tiny borough of Appleby from Lowther.

Entering Parliament through the back door this way was a common practice. Pitt took his seat on January 23. A month later he made his first speech. At the conclusion, Burke was in tears. "He isn't a chip off the old block but the old block itself!" he exclaimed.

Wilberforce was extremely nervous as he rose to speak the first time. He was afraid that the words wouldn't come. But they did. He spoke against the tax laws and felt his speech hadn't gone over very well. Still, it was a beginning! Soon, like other M.P.s, he joined the clubs and began a whirl of social activity.

He liked Goosetree's, a small club in Pall Mall, where about twenty-five of his companions held memberships. He was also active at Boodle's and other places. Being an "independent," he made a point of going to clubs dominated by both Whigs and Tories. On his first visit to Boodle's he won twenty-five guineas from the Duke of Norfolk in a card game. Later, he won £600 at Goosetree's. As he collected his winnings, he found that several losers had difficulty in paying. Embarrassed, he determined never to gamble again.

Lord North's administration did not survive the loss of America. In 1782 he was followed by Lord Rockingham—a crusty man who liked Wilberforce.

"I hear that Rockingham is going to make you a peer," said Pitt over a cup of tea at Goosetree's. "If he does that you'll be in the House of Lords and won't have to run for election!"

"Don't believe everything you hear," replied Wilberforce, flushing. Nevertheless, several tailors approached him and asked for the privilege to measure him for the necessary robes. But within months Rockingham was dead and was succeeded by Shelburne. Wilberforce was popular in London. People love his singing, his wit, and his mimicry. Among his admirers was the Prince of Wales. It was a fast life—but an empty one. "I'm getting bored with all this endless whirl and artificial life," he groused. And sometimes when he read his diary he felt ashamed of the time he was wasting. After a glance at his diary for 1783 he felt a distinct stab of guilt. It read:

Jan. 24. At the House—indifferent day—dined Goosetree's. Banks got drunk and some others. . . . Home and bed before 12.

Feb. 3. Very bad morning—feverish—went in carriage to House—obliged to pair off by the heat; dined Pitt's. Home evening.

Feb. 5. Exceeding rainy bad day. No fever or very little. Missed House. Dined Goosetree's and played billiards afterwards. Home and bed before 12.

Feb. 7. Morning, Philip Green called at 10 and detained me from church—walked—dined Woodly's—afterwards Goosetree's, where supped. Bed at 2 o'clock.

Dec. 2. Up late. Dined Steele, Catch Club. Sandwich. Then opera—Mrs. Crewe there—supped Lord George's—Lord John there. . . . Mrs. Crewe made the party promise to adjourn to Downing Street next night. Bed about 3.

Dec. 3. Dined Goosetree's—played cards and supped Duchess of Portland's. . . . Heavy evening. Bed about 3."

During this period, Wilberforce inherited an eight- or nine-bedroom villa at Wimbledon—just outside London—willed to him by his Methodist uncle. Being in the country and having a spacious garden, it was an ideal spot for those who wanted to escape the city. Pitt frequently stayed for weeks at a time.

The pace here was just as hectic as London. There was often a routine of cards, gambling, practical jokes, elaborate feasts. Often Wilberforce and his guests didn't get to bed until 4:00 a.m.—and frequently later. With both position and wealth, the young M.P. burned his candle at both ends. Barely five feet tall and afflicted with a delicate stomach and feeble eyes, it was all Wilberforce could do to keep up with the routine in which he was entrapped.

Staggering into bed at dawn, his mind often drifted back to his childhood. He remembered the times he had spent in this very house. There had been Bible readings, periods for worship with the servants, visits from Methodist preachers who had come to rest, and long conversations about the purpose of life. He also remembered the hymns—especially those of Charles Wesley, whose "Jesu! Lover of My Soul" kept surging into his memory.

Those had been, by far, the happiest days of his life. He knew his mother approved of the way he was presently living, but he wondered what his uncle and aunt would think if they suddenly returned to life. And he wondered about his previous goal to help the slaves. Was he nearing it, or were those youthful dreams being smothered by social activity?

For a moment Socrates came striding into his vision. Again he could see his fine clothes, the forced smile, the excellent English—and that terrible silver collar. These thoughts were scratching at his brain when he began to smell bacon and eggs. It was time to get up, go to the House, listen to dull speeches—and endure another whirl of social activity. He groaned as he slipped into his clothes.

While bumping toward London in his horse-drawn coach, he thought about Pitt and his remarkable success. At the Windsor coffeehouse his friend had said that his first ambition was to be made Chancellor of the Exchequer—and then Prime Minister. Then it seemed impossible. Now it was half-fulfilled. Prime Minister Shelburne had named him Chancellor of the Exchequer. And Pitt was a mere twenty-three!

Pitt was sparkling as he sat across from Wilberforce at Goosetree's.

"What's the good news?" asked Wilberforce eagerly.

"His Majesty has asked me to become Prime Minister. And—"

"Congratulations! Maybe our time has come to deal with slavery."

"Not yet. I declined the offer."

"You declined! Oh, come now. You must be teasing."

"Yes, I declined. Wilberforce, there's a time for everything, and my time to become the P.M. has not come. When I do become Prime Minister, I want to have enough support in the House to last. Remember, Fox will be on my trail. He has a lot of followers, a lot of ability, and—unfortunately—a lot of influence." He unfolded his starched napkin which was upended like a tower and creased it into a square. Then he cautiously looked around. "Walls have eyes and ears, you know." Satisfied they were alone, he went on:

"Here's the situation. There's been a lot of confusion over the peace treaty with America. Problems about territory and so on. Fox and North have taken advantage of this confusion. On February 14, they got together and formed a coalition. Of course, you know that. . . ."

"Yes, I've been keeping my eyes and ears open," replied Wilberforce. "The thing that amazes me is that the two can get along. I can still remember how Fox used to bore into North when he was the P.M. Fox was never more eloquent than when he was attacking North!"

"True. But Fox claims that their main differences were over the war, and since that mess is now out of the way, they can get along." Pitt motioned for a waiter and ordered more tea.

"I don't know whether you were in the House or not on the seventeenth," continued Pitt. "But as you know, the coalition defeated the Shelburne government by a vote of 224 to 208, and then four days later, they defeated them by a vote of 207 to 190. This, of course, forced Shelburne to resign on the twenty-fourth.

"His majesty is absolutely furious. Shelburne is the one who suggested to the King that he make me Prime Minister. I was tempted, Billy, but I turned it down. I still get chills when I think about it."

King George was so upset over these events, he wrote out his abdication. Later, he thought better of it. By the end of the month his hand was forced by the "total stagnation of Public Business." These realities soon pressed him into doing what he hated. On March 31, Pitt resigned as Chancellor of the Exchequer, and the next day—April 1—the Duke of Portland became Prime Minister, and Fox along with North were given the seals as Secretaries of State.

Disgusted with what had happened, Pitt contacted Wilberforce. "Since I'm out of office," he said, "Eliot—my brother-in-law-to-be—and I are going to France for a long vacation. How about joining us?"

"Of course," agreed Wilberforce. Then, remembering Pitt's neglect of details, he asked, "Do you have a letter of introduction to some key person who can introduce us to those in power?"

"Not yet, but I'll get one."

Pitt contacted his friend Robert Smith and asked him to secure a letter of introduction from Peter Thellusson—a banker. Confident that this letter was all they needed, the three young men set out for France.

At Rheims the trio presented their letter of introduction only to discover that the "key person" was merely a vegetable dealer! He was friendly. But he had no connections with the nobility.

"Let's rent a room and study French," shrugged Wilberforce.

After ten days of study, they persuaded their "host" to take them to the lieutenant of police. In turn, this officer introduced them to the Council of State, Abbé de Lageard. Lageard provided entertainment. He even arranged a stag hunt. And during the hunt, nearsighted Wilberforce nearly shot Pitt.

By the time they got to Fontainebleau—summer quarters of the extravagant French Court—they learned the story of their embarrassment had preceded them. At one of several dinners with Marie Antoinette in the magnificent palace all ablaze with crystal, she teased them. "Have you heard from the vegetable dealer?" she asked, her silvery voice tinkling like ice in a glass.

Jacques Necker, the French Minister of Finance, was

impressed with Pitt. "If you'll marry my daughter," he is reported to have said, "I'll provide her with an income of £14,000 a year."

"That's thoughtful of you," murmured Pitt. "However, I'm already married to my country!"

They visited the Marquis de Lafayette, who had just returned from America, and stopped at the home of Benjamin Franklin—the current rage in Paris. Dr. Franklin—as they honored him in France—was delighted with their call. He shook their hands again and again and beamed at them through the oblong bifocals he had invented. Franklin had been a warm friend of Whitefield's and had printed books against slavery. Wilberforce longed to interview him. But there wasn't time.

The young politicians also visited the Place de la Concorde and had a glimpse of the Bastille. "I shudder whenever I see a political prison like that," said Pitt.

"I know how you feel," returned Wilberforce. "Still it's no worse than our Tower of London. Stopping free speech is always wrong. Always!"

Suddenly a special messenger from England trotted up. "I have an urgent letter for Mr. Pitt," he said.

Quickly Pitt broke the wax seal and unfolded the page. "We must leave for London at once!" he announced crisply.

As the coach bounced on the sometimes treacherous French roads, the trio discussed the politics and political health of France. "I was much impressed with Marie Antoinette," said Wilberforce. "She's extravagant, but she has an enormous sense of humor. And her throat! She has one of the prettiest, swanlike throats I've ever seen."

You shouldn't be noticing women's throats," laughed Pitt.

"What did you think of her husband, King Louis XVI?" asked Eliot.

"He didn't impress me," admitted Wilberforce. "All I can remember is his strange figure and those immense boots. He has sort of a piggish look. I don't think he does anything but eat!"

"France is a sick country," said Pitt thoughtfully. "The nation is practically bankrupt. The American war cost them a lot of money, and their taxes are unfair. The clergy and the nobles don't even have to pay the land tax. But that tax is imposed on the middle and lower classes with a vengeance.

"One of these days there will be a terrible explosion. I'm afraid blood will flow."

"Slavery still has a firm hold," said Wilberforce. "Everyone I talked to seemed to think that slavery is a necessity to their colonies. And the pitiful thing about it is that they are just as indifferent to slavery as the British!"

5
THE ZONG

LESS THAN two months after the trio returned to London, political lightning zigzagged through the House of Commons. On December 18, King George demanded the seals from Fox and North. Twelve hours later, Pitt was summoned to the palace. This time he was ready.

At twenty-four, the slender, six-foot youth was Britain's youngest prime minister!

But it wasn't all glory. When the rather awkward Pepper Arden announced the appointment to the House, the announcement was met with hoots of laughter.

"The King has robbed the cradle," shouted one.

"He won't last a week," sneered another.

Mrs. Crewe, the famous party giver, summed up

public opinion when she remarked, "It will be a mince pie administration."

Pitt knew better than anyone that he could not survive a vote of censure. He felt like a man walking a tightrope stretched between two buildings in the midst of a hurricane. Even before the day was out, Fox and North began to solicit votes and organize their forces to rid the House of this "stripling."

The gamblers in London offered high odds that Pitt's government would fall within thirty days.

Indeed, his office was so insecure, Pitt found it hard to assemble a Cabinet. All the first-class talent refused. No one wanted to board a leaky ship! A Cabinet was finally put together, but it was not an impressive one. It came completely from the House of Lords and included Lord Thurlow, a man he despised.

When Parliament reassembled after Christmas, Fox sauntered over to the opposition side dressed in his formal robes as Secretary of State. Glancing at him sitting there like a lump of clay, his powdered eyebrows slanting toward his triangular hat, Pitt was shaken. He knew Fox had chosen a dramatic way to point out that although he had been dismissed by the King, he was still the House's choice.

"I haven't forgotten reform or slavery," confided Pitt to Wilberforce in a quiet corner at Goosetree's. "But right now it is all I can do to survive. The sword of Damocles hangs over my head. And no one knows when that single hair will break!"

During the next ten days, however, a tiny star of hope began to shimmer. On the sixteenth, Fox brought forward a motion that Pitt's ministry was unconstitutional. The motion carried but only by a narrow margin of twenty-one—not enough to unseat him. A week later, Fox stopped Pitt's India bill. Again, he won. This time, however, by a mere eight votes. Pitt was gaining. Moreover, signs of approval poured in from all over Britain.

About this time the story of the slave ship *Zong* began to reappear in the papers. It was a horror story and its sordid details grabbed the front pages. The reason for the sudden reappearance was the approaching trial in March. Wilberforce clipped the articles and did some personal investigation. He was determined to bring the affair to the attention of William Pitt.

Wilberforce and the Prime Minister were relaxing by the fireplace at Wimbledon when Wilberforce felt the time had come to relate the story of the *Zong*. "Tea will be served in a few minutes," he said. "In the meantime I want to talk about this *Zong* business." He held a stack of clippings close to his eyes and began:

"On September 6, 1781, the *Zong* was ready to sail for Jamaica. It was anchored at the island of St. Thomas, just off the coast of Africa. The Liverpool ship was under the command of Luke Collingwood. There were 470 slaves and seventeen whites on board.

"The ship's holds were so jammed with slaves there was hardly any breathing room. From the time the ship sailed on the sixth, a sickness settled on both crew and slaves. By November 29, sixty blacks and seven whites had died and were thrown overboard.

"On November 29, Captain Collingwood summoned the officers to his cabin for an emergency meeting. 'We have a problem,' he said. 'According to the insurance contract, if the slaves die a natural death it is our loss. But if they are thrown overboard while still alive, the insurance company has to pay. Now, as we all know, the slaves are sick and even if they survive they will not bring a good price. Also, their disease may spread. We've invested a lot of good money in these slaves. What shall we do? Shall we drown them and collect the money or let them die natural deaths and lose even the money we have invested in them?'"

Wilberforce poked the fire and as the sparks blew upward he fingered through the clippings. Finally, toward the bottom of the pile he found what he wanted. "Yes, here is the clause from the policy:

> The insurer takes upon him the risk of the loss, capture, and death of slaves, or any other unavoidable accident to them: but natural death is always understood to be excepted:—by natural death is meant, not only when it happens by disease or sickness, but also when the captive destroys himself through despair, which often happens: *but when slaves are killed, or thrown into the sea in order to quell an insurrection on their part, then the insurers must answer.*"

"That is the most villainous thing I ever heard," exclaimed Pitt, leaping to his feet. "In simple English it means that the captain of a slaver is rewarded in cash for murdering his victims! It is unbelievable, absolutely unbelievable—especially in a Christian nation like ours."

"Oh, but we haven't even got to the heart of the matter," said Wilberforce. "Sit down while I read the rest. When Captain Collingwood suggested that the slaves be thrown into the sea, his chief mate, James Kelsal, objected. But Collingwood managed to persuade Kelsal to do it his way. And so 132 slaves were chosen and dragged to the deck. Fifty-four were thrown to the sharks at once.

"One of the fifty-four, however, managed to get hold

of a rope, climb back on board, and remain hidden. He's now one of the witnesses.

"The next day, forty-two more were drowned, and on the following day, another lot of thirty-six were herded toward the rail. This group resisted and so they were shackled and heaved overboard with the manacles on their legs and wrists. Actually, the crew didn't throw them all overboard, for ten of them broke away and leaped into the sea on their own."

"And where is the captain now?" asked Pitt.

"Collingwood is now in England and is trying to collect from the insurance company. He's demanding £30 per head. He says that he was compelled to throw the slaves overboard because the *Zong* was out of water. The insurance company disputes that. It seems—"

"Someone must be pushing this case," interrupted Pitt, holding up his hand. "Who is it?" he leaned forward eagerly.

"Granville Sharp," replied Wilberforce without a pause.

Pitt frowned. "Isn't he the one who rescued that former slave—let's see—Thomas Lewis from Robert Stapylton?"

"That's right."

"A most interesting man. I met him once. He has a sort of hawklike appearance with deep-set cheeks. I've been told that he's as determined as Satan himself." Pitt laughed.

"I've never had the pleasure of meeting him," admitted Wilberforce. "But since he hates slavery more than anyone I know, I consider him to by my ally. I've made a study of him." The door opened and the butler entered with tea and pastries.

"Like myself, Sharp is a Yorkshireman," said Wilberforce as he poured the tea. "His grandfather was Archbishop of York and his father Archdeacon of Northumberland. But the church wasn't for him. He became an apprentice to a linen dealer. While working at this trade, he got into an argument with a Unitarian.

" 'The reason you don't agree with my theology,' said the Unitarian, 'is that you don't know Greek.' And so do you know what Sharp did?" Wilberforce asked.

"I have no idea," said Pitt.

"Well, he learned Greek—and he learned it on his own. Indeed, he learned it so well he refuted the Unitarian—and then he went on to discover—and prove—some errors in the translation of the New Testament.!"

Pitt reached for a tart. "He must have a brilliant mind."

"He certainly does. After his argument with the Unitarian, he got into another. This time with a rabbi. It was something about Old Testament prophecies. When the argument heated up, the rabbi said, 'Your trouble is that you don't know Hebrew.' "

Wilberforce refilled the Prime Minister's cup. "And do you know what Sharp did?"

"I suppose he learned Hebrew."

"That's right, and again he learned it on his own. Then he—at least according to his own estimation—demolished the argument of the rabbi. Next, he went on to publish a book about his discussion. It is called *Rules Relative to the Hebrew Conversive Vau.*"

"And what else has he done?" asked Pitt with a broad smile.

"Well, he had a friend, a retired tradesman, who claimed that he was legal heir to the title of Lord

Willoughby de Parham. No one believed the old man, for a lot of people make similar claims. But Sharp believed him. He ransacked libraries and practically devoured every book he could find on the subject.

"And do you know what he did?"

"I suppose he put him in the House of Lords," said Pitt, a fresh tart in his hand.

"That's right," laughed Wilberforce. "He's a most unusual man. He's even had the courage to get into an argument with Sam Johnson!"

"He ought to be in the Cabinet," said Pitt, his eyes twinkling.

"No, I don't think he should be in the Cabinet," replied Wilberforce thoughtfully. "Right now he has only one obsession, and that is to rid Britain of slavery. And no one, not even the Prime Minister, should interfere with anyone driven by such an obsession!"

"If you don't hurry and drink some of this tea and eat some of these delicious tarts, you'll go hungry," laughed Pitt. "And while you're doing that, I want to express some of the things that are on my heart." He got up and began to pace back and forth.

"Fox and North are determined to oust me. As you know, Fox has great ability—and a large following. However, the Coalition is supporting policies that are most obnoxious to the King. I saw him recently, and he was very upset and angry. One of these days they'll go too far. And when they do, if I'm still the P.M., I will suggest to His Majesty that he dissolve Parliament and call for a general election. Should that happen, Wilberforce, we will have our greatest opportunity.

"The Coalition doesn't seem to know it, but the voters across England are turning more and more to our side.

The average Englishman still stands behind the King—and don't you forget it!"

"When do you think the crisis will come?"

Pitt made a steepled church with his fingers. "I—I really don't know. But when it comes—and it will come—slavery and reform will have my full attention!"

The case of *Gregson versus Gilbert* (the civil suit over the *Zong*) was heard in the Guildhall, London, on March 6. A horrified, anonymous listener at the trial, wrote an indignant letter and mailed it to *The Morning Chronicle and London Advertizer.* The editors printed it. Wilberforce secured his copy while he was attending a session in the House. As a dull speaker droned on about a technicality, Wilberforce slumped in a corner and read.

"The jury, without going out of court," wrote the unknown correspondent, "gave judgment against the insurance company; the mate [Kelsal] acknowledged he himself had thrown slaves overboard by the captain's order, which he thought was to him a sufficient warrant for any possible thing, without considering whether it was criminal or not.

"The narrative seemed to make everyone present shudder; and I waited with some impatience, expecting that the jury, by their foreman, would have applied to the court for information how to bring the perpetrator of such a horrid deed to justice. . . .

"That there should be bad men to do bad things in all large communities, must be expected; but a community makes the crime general, and provokes divine wrath, when it suffers any member to commit flagrant acts of villainy without punishment.

"The claim of African slaves on the public is exceeding

strong. They owe us no service, they never have received any benefit from us. . . . It is hardly possible for us to thrive when the perpetrator of such complicated guilt as the present, is not only suffered to go unpunished, but is allowed to glory in the infamy, and carries off the reward of it. . . .

"It is certainly worthy of observation that our legislature can every session find time to enquire into and regulate the matter of killing a partridge, that no abuse should be committed, and that he should be fairly shot; and yet it has never thought proper to enquire into the matter of annually kidnapping 50,000 poor wretches, who never injured us, by a set of the most cruel monsters that this country can send out."°

Wilberforce was dabbing at his eyes by the time he had finished. Perhaps when the case was appealed, the decision would be reversed. He hoped that the murderers—for that is what he believed them to be—would be criminally prosecuted. Surely such injustice could not be tolerated in eighteenth-century England!

The insurance company was optimistic that they would not have to pay for the slaves that had been drowned. They felt this way because they had overwhelming evidence that the Zong had not run out of water. Indeed, they were certain they could prove that the ship had arrived in Jamaica on December 22 with 420 gallons of water to spare!

Lord Mansfield set the date for the hearing in the Court of King's Bench on May 21 and 22. This hearing

---

°Quoted from *Black Slaves in Britain* by F. O. Shyllon. Oxford University Press, 1974. I have replaced several archaic words with more modern ones for the sake of clarity.

would determine whether or not a new trial should be granted. At the trial, Davenport, Pigott, and Heywood appeared for the insurance company. The Solicitor General, John Lee, appeared for the owners of the *Zong*.

After counsel for the insurance company had pointed out that the *Zong* had not been in danger because of lack of water or because of leaks, Pigott angrily demanded:

"Is it not strange that the parties concerned should be suffered to go out of the kingdom, when they ought to be tried for murder? . . . I contend that as long as any water remained to be divided, these men were as much entitled to their share as the captain, or any other man whatever."°

To this John Lee was scornful. Said he: "This is the case of *chattels or goods*. . . . It is the case of throwing over *goods*. . . ." In one place in his tirade, he faced Granville Sharp, who had attended all the hearings, and became more vehement than ever. He almost hissed that it would be "madness" to prosecute for murder because "*the blacks were property.*" As for the crew of the *Zong* being guilty of murder, he said: "There is not the least imputation—*of cruelty, I will not say—but of impropriety: not in the least!*"°

Lord Mansfield agreed that there should be a new trial. But there is no record of a new trial being held. In the proceedings, however, Mansfield ruled that the case was as "*if horses had been thrown overboard.*"

Speaking to friends about the matter, Wilberforce exclaimed again and again, "It's impossible for me to believe human beings could be so cruel. The law must be changed!"

°° *Ibid.*

The battle between Pitt and Fox continued. Fox supported a bill on India. It was a complicated one, and although it had some agreeable points it transferred all political power to a board of seven commissioners in London. King George loathed the entire bill and let it be known in the House of Lords that he would consider all who voted for it as his enemies.

Wilberforce joined Pitt in speaking against the bill.

Overnight the drama between the rivals quickened. On February 28 on his way to the city Pitt's carriage was mobbed and he just managed to escape. Fox was accused of instigating the affair. He denied it, and it has never been proved. Still, the incident fanned the crisis to white heat.

"Wilberforce," announced Pitt, his eyes flashing, "we must go to the people! A huge rally has been planned at York for March 25. You're a Yorkshireman and a representative from Hull. And so you are the ideal person to go. I'm counting on you to speak in defense of the King—and this administration. Do your best. In the meantime, I'll try to persuade His Majesty to dissolve Parliament and announce a general election. The weights on the clock have been lifted and it is about to strike."

To be at his best, Wilberforce went to York three days early so that he would have time to rest, get the feel of the situation—and plan. At his inn he drew a line down the center of a sheet of paper and listed the good points and the bad points of an election.

He knew that Pitt was uncomfortable in being a representative from Appleby. This was both because it was a "rotten borough" and because of the way the seat had been presented to him by Sir James Lowther.

How was he to speak effectively against pocket boroughs and borough-mongers if he had benefited by them? A general election could eliminate that problem. This he knew, for on his way to York he had gone through Cambridge, and there one of the important men had asked if Pitt would stand for them at the next election.

He was confident a general election would defeat many North and Fox men and give Pitt a solid or, perhaps, an overwhelming majority. He was also confident that he could be reelected at Hull.

He was walking around the block, enjoying the sunshine, when it suddenly occurred to Wilberforce that he ought to stand for the County of York. He had casually thought of this before, but never seriously. If he had been drinking, he'd have blamed the thought on alcohol. The County of York seat was the most coveted one in the House!

Excitedly, he went back to the inn and got out the sheet of paper where he had listed the advantages of an election. Quickly he began to figure. It had cost him between £8000 and £9000 to win the 1,126 votes at Hull. However, to win at York he would have to receive a minimum of 12,000 votes, and that many votes at £8 each would cost him nearly £100,000! Thoughts of spending that much money startled him. He started to crumble the paper. Then he stopped. Perhaps there was another way!

Since 1779, a new influence had arisen in York in the form of the Yorkshire Association. This association of leading men was dedicated to reform. If he could get them to propose him as the County of York representative, he would have a chance. Such an idea, however, did not seem practical, since these aristocratic people wanted a candidate from one of the great landed families. He was merely the son of a merchant!

Nevertheless, there was a chance—a very slight chance—that if his speech gripped the crowd, he might be the man. Wilberforce paced the streets as the thoughts of this "mad scheme" warmed his brain. Quickly, dramatic phrases for his forthcoming speech leaped into his head. He remembered the Methodists taught that men should lose themselves in a cause bigger than themselves. Well he had such a cause—the cause of slavery!

Ah, but what if the King did not dissolve Parliament and the coalition was enabled to force Pitt out of office? The thought sickened him. Perhaps there would be a letter from Pitt at the desk. The clerk shook his head. "The mail has come. There's nothing for you. Sorry."

March 25 was a cold, shivering day. Hail pounded into the streets and the winds tugged at the wooden canopy in the castle yard where the rally was scheduled to be held from 10:00 a.m. until 4:30 p.m. Before leaving the inn, Wilberforce checked at the desk. Again the clerk shook his head. "The mail came from London. But there's nothing for you."

Wilberforce started to leave and then he stopped. "If a letter comes while I'm speaking," he said, "I'd be grateful if you'd sent it over by special messenger. It's extremely important."

The castle yard was jammed with an immense crowd. Wilberforce struggled with the wind as he forced himself toward the wooden canopy. The wind ruffled his hair and snatched at his coat. With difficulty, he climbed the steps and took a seat behind the speaker's table. As he peered over the table through his nearsighted eyes, two fears gripped his heart: (1) he feared the many speakers ahead of him would tire the people and they would drift away and (2) he was afraid the weather might worsen to the point the meeting would have to be dismissed. Even then, the wind was flinging the speaker's words back into his teeth.

Soon a statement to the King which condemned the Coalition was read. The statement was seconded for adoption by Mr. H. Duncombe, Mr. Baynes, Mr. Milnes, Mr. Stanhope, and Lord Fauconberg. Speaking in opposition were Lord Surrey, Lord Carlisle, Lord Cavendish, and Lord Fitzwilliam. Wilberforce gritted his teeth.

As far as rank was concerned, it was a lopsided contest!

Finally, William Wilberforce mounted the table. From a distance he seemed a pitiful sight. He resembled a sparrow with its feathers blowing out. The edge of the crowd began to thin. Wilberforce took a deep breath and began. From the first sentence, the crowd was held by the magic of his voice. He was well into his speech when a frantic messenger puffed up to the platform with a letter. He shoved it at Wilberforce.

The man had ridden a horse from London and the trip had taken two days. The letter was from William Pitt. It informed Wilberforce that Parliament had been dissolved and it advised him to "keep all our friends together and to tear the enemy to pieces."

After no more than a thirty-second pause, Wilberforce announced that Parliament had been dissolved and that the King was appealing to the nation. From this point on, his eloquence reached new heights. The crowd was riveted to the ground as the twenty-four-year-old orator carried them from one climax to another.

Later on, James Boswell reported the scene to Henry Dundas. "I saw," said the biographer of Sam Johnson, "what seemed a mere shrimp mount upon the table; but as I listened, he grew, and grew, until the shrimp became a whale."

Following the meeting, Whigs and Tories, Lords and merchants, Associators and non-Associators, crowded together to select their candidates. There were angry words, tense moments, threats—and laughter. But at midnight there was a spontaneous shout, "Wilberforce and liberty!"

Campaign money was raised and a vigorous campaign launched. A thorough canvass, however, indicated to both sides that Wilberforce was the desired man, and so the opposition withdrew. There was no merit in fighting a lost cause.

Wilberforce was now a representative from the County of York!

Likewise, the landslide election favored Pitt. He won a seat from Cambridge and 160 members of the coalition were defeated. Indeed, the Coalition was so heavily battered, the losers were dubbed "Fox martyrs"!

The polls for Fox's own election to the seat at Westminster were open for forty days. At the close of each day, Fox inquired where he stood. By the end of the tenth day, he was trailing by 318 votes. His workers employed every device to get out voters for him. Even the Prince of Wales came to his aid. In the end, he squeaked through as a winner. Nevertheless, Fox had been humiliated.

6
CONVERSION

FOR MONTHS, Elizabeth Wilberforce had been insisting that her son—now the distinguished M.P. from York—accompany her on a long trip on the continent. The grind of politics had hindered; but now that Parliament was recessed, Wilberforce was eager to go.

Since his mother had invited his sister and two female cousins to come along, Wilberforce decided there must be two carriages. Traveling with four women in the same coach was too much—even for him! At the same time he didn't want to occupy an entire coach all by himself. And so he approached his friend, W. Burgh.

"It will be a pleasant trip," he explained. "We'll travel slowly, eat well, and see the country."

"I'm sorry, Mr. Wilberforce," replied Burgh, shaking his head. "I can't possibly go. Some other time...."

Almost accidentally Wilberforce bumped into Isaac Milner at Scarsdale. Milner had been his teacher at the Hull Grammar School, and since then he had won many honors. When he took his degree in Cambridge in 1774 he had been named Senior Wrangler, and given the distinction of being "incomparabilis." And even better than this, he was a marvelous storyteller, and his stories were additionally salty because of his broad, Yorkshire accent. To him, little was "latle" and school was "skiewl."

The important thing Wilberforce forgot—or didn't seriously consider—was that Milner was a celebrated preacher!

"I'd love to go with you," said Milner, peering down at him, "even though we'll make an odd pair." It was an interesting comment, for he was physically huge—a human mountain. A friend remembered, "He was the most enormous man it was my fate to see in a drawing room." In comparison, Wilberforce was a mere foothill. Moreover, Milner ate three times as much as a normal person. At every restaurant the waiters were goggle-eyed.

The two carriages crossed France to Lyons, boarded a luxurious ship, and floated down the Rhone to Avignon. From here they went overland to Aix and then sailed down to Marseilles, where Wilberforce noticed a trio of slavers at anchor. At Avignon, a cousin overheard Lady Rivers discussing Wilberforce. "He's all soul and no body," she shrilled. Another tourist was certain he would die at Nice!

Riding with Milner was great fun. Wilberforce relived school days. "I can never forget how your brother stood me on a table and made me orate. It was embarrassing. But I'm sure he's the one who got me interested in public speaking," remembered Wilberforce.

Milner was stuffed with the latest knowledge—especially in the field of mathematics. Wilberforce enjoyed picking his brains. He would ask such questions as who should be given credit for inventing the digit zero. And both were intrigued that they were in the land of Antoine Lavoisier—the chemist who had just proved that fire consumes oxygen as it burns.

As they followed the difficult roads toward Nice, Milner kept bringing up the subject of Christianity. Each time Wilberforce turned the conversation to something else with a clever—often flippant—answer. Christianity—particularly that of the evangelical type—had no more appeal to him than a year-old crust of bread. The exotic life of London and his recent election had dimmed the memory of his youthful days with the Methodists. Still, Christianity was on his mind. In spite of himself, he kept bringing it up.

"I'm no match for you, Wilberforce," exclaimed Milner, throwing up his gigantic arms. "But if you want to discuss these subjects seriously, I will gladly do so." before leaving Nice on February 5, a date Wilberforce was to remember, he casually picked up the book, *Rise and Progress of Religion* by Philip Doddridge.

The book had come to him in a rather roundabout way. Mrs. Unwin, friend of hymn writer William Cowper, had given it to the mother of one of the cousins. She, in turn, had slipped it into her suitcase.

"What do you think of it?" asked Wilberforce, a trifle smugly.

"It's one of the best books written," replied Milner

warmly. "Let's take it along and study it on the journey."

"That will be fine," agreed Wilberforce, stifling a yawn. His mind was on a distant snow-covered peak.

The roads were all but impassable and were made worse by eighteen days of snow in the Alps. At one place the hill they were ascending was so treacherous, the two sloshed through the snow on foot. And then it happened.

The weight of their carriage overpowered the horses, and it hung precariously on the edge of a precipice. Milner saw the danger just in time. With his Atlas-like strength he got the carriage back on the road. He and Wilberforce then wrapped themselves in their traveling bags and continued to study Doddridge.

Soon Wilberforce was back in London. Again it was Goosetree's, Boodle's, the House, dinner with Pitt, the theater, Opera, dancing, cards—and politics. Pitt was determined to disfranchise thirty-six rotten boroughs and turn their seats over to London and the counties. Wilberforce worked with him, but most of their efforts ended in disappointment. Parliament wasn't ready for reform!

Had the reading of Doddridge changed Wilberforce? Not on the outside. But his diary began to show inward change. An entry read: "Dined Hamilton's—christening—very indecent—all laughing around." Another—dated April 14—was even more revealing: "opera—shocking dance of Festin de Pierre, and unmoved audience. S and I talked—strange that the most generous men and religious, do not see that their duties increase with their fortune, and that they will be punished for spending it in eating, etc."

Again Wilberforce and Milner went to the continent.

This time they took along the Greek New Testament which they studied together. And now Wilberforce began to change. Again, the first indication of this change was in the diary. On November 24, he wrote:

> Heard the Bible read two hours—Pascal one hour and a quarter—meditation one hour and a quarter—business the same. . . .

On September 27, he continued in the same mood:

> I must awake to my dangerous state, and never be at rest until I have made my peace with God. My heart is so hard, my blindness so great, that I cannot get a due hatred of sin, though I see I am all corrupt, and blinded to the perception of spiritual things.

Wilberforce desperately needed help. But where was he to go? His spiritual hero, George Whitefield, had died in America in 1770. And the Established Church in England was almost a mockery. Churches and bishoprics were passed out to helpful friends by politicians. Many pastors never visited their congregations. Indeed, some of them seldom bothered to even preach, and Sam Johnson was reported to have remarked that he had never met a religious clergyman.

In pondering where to seek help, Wilberforce suddenly remembered the colorful John Newton—a former slaver. Research provided a thumbnail sketch of the man. The son of a sea captain who sailed the Mediterranean, Newton went to sea in his youth. In his teens, he knew nothing of discipline. Thus he jumped ship, was flogged, and on several occasions almost drowned. Finally, he became a slaver. During a storm he nearly lost his life, and decided for Christ. But even though he was an earnest

Christian, he continued to transport slaves from Guinea to the West Indies. He evidently did this with a clear conscience. In fact, he often lingered on his knees with the open Bible in front of him and hundreds of shackled slaves a few inches below the carpet.

Finally, he became a preacher. In this position, he began to loathe slavery and to fight it with every ounce of strength he possessed. Newton's life had been so changed, he often signed his letters "The Old African Blasphemer."

Wilberforce paced the floor as he considered whether or not he should go to Newton. After long consideration, he dated a sheet of paper December 2, 1785. He then dipped his quill and wrote:

Sir,
    There is no need of apology for intruding on you, when the errand is religion. I wish to have some serious conversation with you, and will take the liberty of calling on you for this purpose, in half an hour; when, if you cannot receive me, you will have the goodness to let me have a letter put into my hands at the door, naming a time and place for our meeting, the earlier the more agreeable to me.
I have had ten thousand doubts within myself, whether or not I should discover myself to you; but every argument against doing it has its foundation in pride. I am sure you will hold yourself bound to let no one living know of this application, or of my visit, till I release you from the obligation.
    P.S. Remember that I must be secret, and that the gallery of the House is now so universally attended, that the face of a member of Parliament is pretty well known.

He folded the sheet of paper and personally took it to the church on Sunday, December 4, and delivered it himself to Newton.

An appointment was made for the following Wednesday. Wilberforce was so nervous about the whole affair he completely walked around the square not only once but a second time before he had the courage to knock at Newton's study.

But the former slaver soon put him at ease. "I had been praying and believing that you'd come," he said, his pink, round face shining beneath his freshly powdered wig.

The young M.P. felt his heart race as he glanced around the study. It contained the usual row of books—heavy volumes by Luther, Calvin, Augustine, and Wesley. There were also several well-worn maps.

"T-tell me about that one," managed Wilberforce. He nervously pointed to a large map of Northwest Africa.

"That's Guinea," said Newton. "Guinea supplies most of the slaves of the world." He held the map close to the light at the window. "It stretches from the Senegal River in the north to Cape Lopez, just south of the equator." Hanging his head, he added, "I'm sorry to admit that I know the place all too well."

"Where is the Bite of Benin?" asked Wilberforce, peering closely.

"So you've heard of that!" Newton's eyes twinkled. "The Bite is right here at the bottom of the bulge." He put a heavy finger on the mouths of the Niger River. "It takes its name from the city of Benin which used to be the capital of this area. Some call it Nigeria. Several strong civilizations have existed there. Indeed, they have some petty kings even now. I know. I've dealt with them and they are tyrants. Have you heard the old sailor rhyme about Benin?"

Wilberforce frowned. "I don't remember. And yet—"

"It's popular among the slavers. It goes like this:

> Beware and take care of the Bite of Benin,
> Few come out, though many go in."

"And why is that?" asked Wilberforce, seating himself.

"There are many reasons. It's a popular place to pick up slaves. You see there are dozens of tribes along the coast. Each tribe has a distinct dialect and set of customs. One tribe scars their faces one way and another tribe scars their face another way. This makes it easier for the slaver because the tribes have old smoldering hatreds. All the slaver has to do is to persuade one village chief to raid his neighbor. He then buys captives from both sides. They also enjoy kidnapping one another.

"I know what it's like, for I often went up the river in a longboat to buy slaves. People who buy and sell other humans get very calloused. Some sink so low they don't seem to possess a conscience." He got up and paced around. "I knew a man who used to tie stones around his unsalable slaves and then fling them into the river for the crocodiles.

"Another slaver had a number of black wives. When he discovered one was having an affair with a slave, he jammed them both in a tar barrel and burned them alive. Those degraded enough to become slavers often get to drinking, knifing one another–and committing suicide. The place is honeycombed with disease—every plague known to Europe, and dozens more. Blackwater fever, yaws, malaria. I know from experience. Many times I was near death. And that's the reason for the line: 'Few come out, though many go in.' "

He dropped into his large, leather-covered seat. "Ah, but you didn't come to discuss slavery. What's on your mind? Maybe I can help." He smiled and waited.

"You've already helped me," said Wilberforce.

"How's that?"

"Well, you were a slaver. You blasphemed, you stole and you drank, and yet you've overcome your past. What's the secret?"

Newton picked up a book and handed it to him. "Do you know what this is?"

"Of course! It's *Olney Hymns*."

"This hymnal has a story which may be helpful. As the world knows, William Cowper has had mental trouble. When I first knew him, he had just emerged from an insane asylum. His trouble was that he was unusually sensitive and was convinced his soul was lost.

"While in the asylum, he read the story of Lazarus. You know, how Jesus raised him from the dead. Seeing the overwhelming love of Christ, Cowper began to improve. After his discharge, he came to see me and I kept him busy in the church. He secured rooms with Mrs. Unwin and we had great fellowship, even though he often reverted to his terrible melancholy.

"Soon Cowper and I decided to write a hymnal. This book is the result. Now listen to one of Cowper's verses." Newton read with gentle emphasis:

> E're since by faith I saw the stream
>   Thy flowing wounds supply,
> Redeeming love has been my theme,
>   And shall be till I die.

"That, Wilberforce, is the testimony of a man who

never went into deep sin." He quickly turned the page. "Now would you like to hear the testimony of one who wallowed in the depths?"

Wilberforce merely nodded, for a lump in his throat had stopped his speech.

"Then listen to this." Newton stood and with eyes closed sang:

> Through many dangers, toils, and snares,
> I have already come:
> 'Tis grace hath bro't me safe thus far,
> And grace will lead me home.

When he finished, huge tears were coursing down his cheeks. "I wrote that," he said, a hand cupping his chin. "It's my own story and I know it's true." He wiped his eyes and the tone of his voice changed. "Since you have a Methodist background I don't have to explain that Cowper's hymn simply means that we are saved by having faith that the blood of Christ, spilled on the cross, pays the price of our sins. All of them! Nor do I have to tell you that the *grace* in my hymn refers to God's unmerited favor."

"Yes, I understand," said Wilberforce. "My problem is that success has led me away from the simplicity of the cross. When I was a lad I was converted. Now I must leave." He unlatched the door.

"One more word," said Newton in a fatherly way. "African kings always wondered how we guided our ships across the ocean. I explained that it was by the use of the compass. But this was beyond their understanding.

"Now even as the stars and the compass guide the captains, God has given us His Word and the Holy Spirit to guide us. God has called you to a great work. And always when He does this, He allows troubles to plague and hinder. I suppose the reason is that He wants us to grow. If you will keep your eyes on the Word and the spiritual compass, you will eventually emerge from every fog and every storm. I shall keep praying for you!"

7
CRUSADE

"WILBERFORCE, I have an important subject I wish to discuss with you," said Pitt abruptly in the summer of 1787. "Let's go outside. We must have privacy!"

This encounter, which turned out to be one of the great meetings in the history of slavery, took place at Holbrook House—the beautiful estate in Kent, which Pitt had purchased two years before. Wilberforce later remembered that Pitt led him and another guest, Samuel Grenville, "to the root of an old tree . . . just above the steep descent into the vale of Keston."*

As they relaxed beneath the clouds, the Prime Minister

---

*The tree survives to this day and is known as "Wilberforce's Oak."

said, "I want you to give notice to the House of Commons that you intend to bring forward the subject of slavery." He hesitated. And then, looking Wilberforce full in the face, added, "Others have wanted to do this. But you are the best prepared and I think you are the right man.

"Ridding Britain of this curse will be hard. The battle will require all the courage, tact, and stamina you possess. But I believe you can manage. What is your answer?"

Wilberforce had written a long letter to Pitt about his conversion. In it, he had explained that because of his change of views he could no more be so much a "party man" as he had been before. Pitt had replied with an affectionate letter assuring him that he still respected him and that they could work together. Moreover, he had signed the letter "Believe me, affectionately and unalterably yours, W. Pitt."

Following this, they had had a two-hour conversation in which they had remained in disagreement about Christianity. But now this request indicated that the old ties which had bound them together had not been broken.

Wilberforce replied, "British slavery is as deeply entrenched as a wisdom tooth. Removing it will not be easy. Parliament is filled with men who have investments in the business. Getting rid of slavery will be a terrible battle. Men will lose their seats. Friendships will be broken. But, Mr. Prime Minister, I'm ready. Since my conversion I've found that I have vast spiritual resources. God will help!"

The two young men—both a mere twenty-eight—shook hands over their covenant. For a time Wilberforce had considered resigning from Parliament and entering the ministry. Now, he realized that he already had a ministry: the ministry of abolition!

After his conversion, Wilberforce sold his house at Wimbledon. He felt that he should no longer "waste" his time in this country place as he had previously done. He moved to a large house in Palace Yard. It was an ideal headquarters for the battle ahead. One evening Thomas Clarkson called on him.

"Come in!" greeted Wilberforce with enthusiasm. "It's been several days since I've seen you. Have a seat." He and Clarkson had much in common. Both had attended St. John's at Cambridge, were about the same age, and were deeply religious. Clarkson's father was a preacher. In addition, both hated slavery.

Clarkson seated himself across from Wilberforce. "I— I have something important I want to discuss with you," he said, a little uncomfortably. His round handsome face was unusually taut.

"Yes?" said Wilberforce gently.

"It's— It's— It's—" His speech stuttered to a stop.

"Don't be nervous," encouraged Wilberforce. He shook a little brass bell. "I'll have the butler bring some tea. That'll perk you up." He waited for the painful moment as the speechless Clarkson stared at the rug. "I'll be glad to help you if I can. Don't be afraid. . . ."

In response, Clarkson suddenly leaped to his feet. "I— I must be on my way," he said, as he fled out the door.

Puzzled, Wilberforce began to piece together those things he knew about Clarkson.

In 1785, Dr. Peckard, a teacher at Cambridge, offered a prize for the best essay on the subject "Is It Right to

Make Men Slaves Against Their Will?" At the time, Clarkson knew almost nothing about slavery. But he determined he would learn all he could and win the prize. He thought his chances were pretty good since he had won the first prize in a Latin essay contest the year before.

Clarkson rummaged through libraries and studied every book he could find on slavery, and whenever he met persons who had any knowledge on the subject he grilled them unmercifully. He kept a candle burning by his bedside so that he could jot down any useful thoughts that came to him at night. The more he studied, the more intrigued he became. Soon he was so overcome by the thoughts of slavery that he could not sleep.

While riding his horse to London, he dismounted near Wades Mill in Hertfordshire and sat down to rest. As he rested it occurred to him, as he later put it, "that if the contents of this essay were true, it was time some person should see these calamities to their end." With this thought churning his mind, he reached home consumed with a determination. He then worked harder than ever on the essay.

The essay won first prize. Normally, this would have been the end of the affair. But he had a feeling that this was just the beginning of his career. He decided to translate his essay from Latin into English. Perhaps the English version would stir up some interest.

He approached Mr. Cadell in the Strand with the idea of publishing it. Cadell was enthusiastic. He said, "Since the essay has been honored by the University of Cambridge with the first prize, it should enjoy a respectable circulation among *persons of taste*."

The words "persons of taste" disturbed Clarkson. He

was not interested in such people. He wanted to reach those who would do something about slavery! By chance, he met a Quaker, Joseph Hancock, at the Royal Exchange.

"I have been wishing to see thee for a long time," said Hancock.

"So?" replied Clarkson.

"Yes, I have been wondering why thou hast not published the essay on slavery. It would do much good."

When Clarkson explained that that was exactly what he wanted to do, Hancock introduced him to a James Phillips, who published the work. This contact opened the way for him to be introduced to Granville Sharp and a group of Quakers who had organized themselves into a committee in 1783. The aim of this committee was "for the relief and liberation of Negro slaves in the West Indies and for the discouragement of the slave trade on the coast of Africa."

As Clarkson hurried away from the home of Wilberforce, he was puzzled at why he had been tongue-tied. Wondering what he should do, he called on Bennet Langton, a member of the Committee, a famous London host, and a close friend of Sam Johnson. "We'll solve the problem easy enough," assured Langton. "We'll invite him along with others to a dinner here in my home and then bring up the subject of slavery."

Upon entering the posh Langton home, Wilberforce was introduced to Sir Charles Middleton, Sir Joshua Reynolds, Mr. Windham, Hawkins Browne—and James Boswell. After dinner, the subject of slavery was discreetly worked into the conversation.

Sir Charles had been the commander of a man-of-war

and while at sea had come upon a slave ship in which an epidemic was raging. Since James Ramsay, his skilled surgeon, was the only medical man available, Dr. Ramsey boarded the stricken ship and did what he could for the slaves. Following his sea days, Ramsay was ordained and served in St. Kitts for nineteen years. During this time, he had seen slaves beaten to death, left to die on the quays, and treated as the lowest species of animals.

After years in St. Kitts, Ramsay accepted a pastorate in England. Sir Charles then succeeded in coaxing him to write a book about his experiences. *Essays on the Treatment of, and Traffic in, Slaves* was the first eyewitness account of slavery in the Caribbean. It caused a sensation.

"Since I'm a member of Parliament," said Sir Charles, "I would like to champion the cause of the slaves. But I'm a seaman and a farmer—not an orator. I'd be a hindrance."

Sir Joshua Reynolds, England's leading portrait painter, had lost his hearing and the sight of one eye. As the discussion went on, he kept turning his ear trumpet from one speaker to the next.

James Boswell seemed uncomfortable. He squirmed and adjusted his wig as evidence was produced against the Trade. His lips twitched as his impatience reached the boiling point. Finally he exploded like a lid on a teakettle. "I think the blacks are far happier as slaves than they are in their own primitive state in Africa," he said somewhat pompously.

Following a stunned silence, Wilberforce remarked, "Maybe so, but we have no right to make people happy against their will!"

His retort inspired a gale of laughter. But from the corner of his eye Wilberforce noticed that Boswell's scowl had deepened.

Toward the close of the evening, Clarkson turned to Wilberforce and a new quiet settled over the group. "My friends and I are deeply committed to the total abolition of slavery," he said. "We have been working hard and have accumulated a lot of evidence. Personally, I put in sixteen hours a day. But we need someone to represent us in Parliament.

"We've watched you and we heard about your famous speech at York. Would you be willing to work with us, to be our voice in the House?"

"I will be glad to do so," said Wilberforce, "provided you can't find anyone better." He considered revealing his promise to Pitt at Holbrook House, but decided against it. There would be opportunity for them to learn that later.

As the guests were leaving, Clarkson drew Wilberforce to one side. "Do you mind if I speak of our agreement in the city?" he asked.

"Certainly not," replied Wilberforce.

Delighted with the results of the meeting, Thomas Clarkson began campaigning to form a committee to work for abolition. Remembering the previous committee, he called on them to enlist their support. Soon the new committee was formed. It consisted of:

Granville Sharp	John Lloyd	John Barton
William Dillwyn	Joseph Woods	Joseph Hooper
Samuel Hoare	Thomas Clarkson	James Phillips
George Harrison	Richard Phillips	Philip Sansom

All the members of this committee were Quakers except for Clarkson, Sharp, and Sansom. Sharp was elected chairman.

After the formation of the Committee, word of what had been done was sent to Wilberforce. And from then on the Committee kept in constant contact with him. One of the first decisions that had to be made concerned what the Committee wanted to abolish.

"I think we should abolish slavery and all of its ramifications!" said Sharp, heatedly. "God will help us, and God can do anything."

"We're all for that," replied Clarkson calmly. "But if we try to accomplish too much all at once, we may not succeed in accomplishing anything."

"Well spoken," agreed another. "If we immediately try to abolish slavery we will run into the subject of property. Remember that lots of people—including many in Parliament—have most of their assets tied up in slaves. Such people would demand compensation. I think we should first aim to abolish the Trade. If we could do that, it would force the planters to take better care of their slaves."

The Committee decided to spend their energies agitating against the Trade.

Wilberforce was delighted with the way things were moving. Pitt assured him that he could count on his support. Realistically, he realized that he would have to work hard to master the entire subject of slavery. He decided that he could not waste a single minute. With this thought in mind, he approached his tailor.

"I want you to put as many extra pockets in my clothes as possible," he said. "And make them big enough to carry books."

"But, Mr. Wilberforce, that's not in the fashion!" objected the man, so alarmed he almost dropped his scissors.

"That doesn't matter. Life is short, and I must keep busy."

From this time on, Wilberforce was a walking library.

He also became concerned with the passage of time. And thinking back over the methods used by Whitefield and the Wesleys, he decided on a method of his own. He drew up a chart that indicated what he did every moment of the day. With this chart hanging in a conspicuous place, he managed his life with the utmost efficiency.

Here is one of his charts:

	Major Application Study.	Minor application Study.	Requisite company, &c. Visits, &c.	Unaccounted for, &c. Dressing.	Relaxation sua causa.	Squandered.	Serious reading, and meditation.	Bed.	Total	House of Commons, business, &c. Left out of plan
Jan. 26th.		5¾	1¾	1¼	¼	½	1½	8½	24	4½
— 27th.			1	½	¼	2¼	1	8½	24½	11
8 28.th			8	¾			½	9¼	24	5½
— 29th.			5½	¼		1	¾	8¼	23½*	7½
— 30th.			8	1			¾	7¾	24	6½
— 31st.			7	½	¼	3¼	¾	9½	25	3¾
Sunday Feb. 1st.			4½	1	¼		8½	8¼	22½	
— 2nd.			3¾	½	¼	2¼	¾	8¼	24¾	8½
— 3rd.			4½	¼			¾	9	23¾	9¼
— 4th.			8¾	1¼			¾	8	24	5¼

Not being a mathematical genius like Pitt, he made a quarter of an hour error on January 29!

On February 11, 1788, King George excited Wilberforce and the committee by decreeing that a *Committee of Privy Council* should investigate the *African Slave Trade*. Deeply challenged, Wilberforce increased his supply of candles. And night after night as they flickered by his bed he memorized endless statistics about the Trade.

Soon his old intestinal problem flared up. This time the attacks were so severe he was confined to bed. While in this condition, Thomas Clarkson stopped to see him. "I'm sorry that I'm stricken," Wilberforce managed, holding out a weak hand. "I—I do hope I don't have to drop out of the fight. . . ." Then with great effort he pointed to his books and the notes he had taken.

"We must prepare well," he muttered through determined lips. "The opposition we'll face is utterly unbelievable. Pitt's Cabinet isn't even agreed. Get all the evidence you can. And then check it, double-check it, and check it again. You and I have Christian scruples about lying. The slavers don't. In addition they're getting rich and none of them want to give up the business. Some may even lie to prove you wrong when you mount the witness stand."

"No doubt you're right, Mr. Wilberforce," said Clarkson. "It wouldn't be the first time in my years as an investigator. Please pray for me. A lot of my work will be in Liverpool, and since I am a native of that city, I'll be easily recognized—an easy target for mischief. Nevertheless, I'll manage. God will help me."

As Clarkson left, Wilberforce could see that he was discouraged. It was evident that Clarkson feared Wilberforce would not recover. Fearful himself, he read from his New Testament and then pinched out the candle.

"O, God," he prayed, "give me the strength I'll need."

8
DIMENSIONS OF HELL

FROM BITTER EXPERIENCE, Clarkson knew that his evidence would have to be as definite and convincing as the multiplication table. A recent experience had emphasized this.

After reading his book on slavery, Lord Lilford was extremely doubtful. "Name one of your doubts," challenged Clarkson.

"I'm concerned about this story of the *Zong*," said Lilford. He pursed his lips and shook his head. "It's frightful! I find it impossible to believe that human beings—Englishmen at that—would toss 132 innocent slaves to the sharks in order to be reimbursed by an insurance company."

Instead of arguing, Clarkson went to Granville Sharp and borrowed the shorthand reports he had had made of the trial. These reports so convinced the lord they turned him into an abolitionist.

Toward the beginning of the new investigation, Clarkson met Alexander Falconbridge, a weather-beaten surgeon who had completed four slaving voyages to Africa.

"I need information about the Trade," said Clarkson, hopefully.

Without a quibble, Falconbridge replied that since he was no longer in the business, he would tell him anything he wanted to know. And since he was physically strong, he volunteered to be Clarkson's bodyguard (The slavers in Liverpool along with investors who benefited from slavery were becoming increasingly hostile. They sneered at Clarkson as a "mad dog" and tried to scare him away with threats of violence.)

While tramping the streets near the docks, Clarkson chanced on a store that catered to slavers. In it, he saw shelves filled with handcuffs, iron collars, thumbscrews, leg-shackles—and a grisly instrument called a *speculum oris*.

"It's first quality merchandise," said the owner eagerly. He was an old man with long hairs sprouting from the rims of his oyster shell ears. "On your way to Guinea?"

"I'll be needing them soon," said Clarkson.

While in the living room of his apartment on the third floor at the inn, Clarkson asked Falconbridge to explain the purpose of the sepculum oris. The doctor picked up the instrument which resembled a heavy carpenter's compass and slowly opened the sharp ends.

"Often the slaves are determined to starve themselves to death," he said. "Normally, a short application of the cat-o'-nine-tails changes their minds. However, a few are so stubborn that doesn't work even though their backs are flogged until they resemble a harrowed field. In that case, the captain resorts to something else." He walked to the window and glanced outside. "I've seen a shovel of glowing coals put so close to their lips they were scorched. The fire generally has the desired effect. When it doesn't, the speculum oris is used." He shuddered and sighed. "This instrument is something that should make us all ashamed!

"The slaves are stretched out on the deck and these points are hammered between their teeth. Next, the screw is slowly twisted. This spreads the ends and thus forces their mouths open. A funnel is then inserted in their mouths and the food is poured in.

"If this fails, thumbscrews are employed. Here, let me show you." He opened the set and Clarkson placed his thumbs inside. Falconbridge then began to screw them shut. "You can see how painful it is. If I were to turn the screw another time or two the blood would spurt and you'd be screaming."

"Do the slaves suffer much during the Middle Passage?" asked Clarkson. "You know some of the captains speak of the trip as a joyous holiday."

"Do they suffer?" exclaimed Falconbridge. "Asking that is like asking if there's salt in the ocean!" He got up and as he shuffled back and forth the words streamed from his lips in torrents.

"The hardships suffered by Negroes during the passage can scarcely be conceived. They're affected by seasickness far more than Europeans and frequently die from it. Lack of fresh air is an intolerable problem. Most ships in the slave trade have five or six airports between decks on each side of the ship. These are about six inches long and four inches wide. In addition a few ships—about one in twenty—have what they call windsails. But whenever the sea is rough it is necessary to shut these. Without fresh air, the holds become intolerably hot. The same confined air, heavily laden with body odor, and breathed again and again, soon produces fevers and fluxes which cause many more to die.

"During the voyages I made, I witnessed many times the fatal effects of the lack of fresh air. On several occasions bad weather caused the portholes to be shut and the grating to be covered. Sickness broke out among the Negroes. Although I tried to go down and look after them, their rooms became so extremely hot I could only bear to remain for a short time.

"But the heat was not the only thing that made their situation intolerable. The floor of their rooms was so covered with the blood and mucous produced by the flux, that it resembled a slaughterhouse. It is not in the power of human imagination to picture a situation more dreadful or disgusting. Many of the slaves fainted. They were carried up to the deck where several died. I myself was so overcome with the heat, stench, and foul air I nearly fainted. It was only with assistance that I could get on deck. I soon fell sick of the same disorder."

Clarkson, himself, was nearly sick after this conversation. But he took notes and verified each point with Falconbridge. In his heart he knew that emotional stories would never move the Privy Council. Statistics were what he wanted, and so he went after them with complete concentration. During this search he had a remarkable break. In September 1887, he received a letter from George Rose. The letter had been relayed to him by Wilberforce. It said:

> It is quite unprecedented to allow anyone to rummage the custom house papers for information who have no employment in the revenue; I will, however, without delay obtain for Mr. Clarkson all the information he wants though I am a West Indian planter, would I were not!

Clarkson took full advantage of this privilege. Before he was through, he had learned the names and histories of 20,000 seamen. Indeed, he and other investigators worked so hard they knew more about slavery than the slavers themselves!

The evidence began to stack up in Wilberforce's library. Each bit was carefully noted and filed in an appropriate place. Wilberforce had long wondered how the captains secured the slaves and so he carefully went into the matter. He especially was anxious to discover the percentage of those who had been kidnapped. He was interested in this because he knew the captains would argue that most of their slaves, if not all, were prisoners of war or condemned cirminals, and thus fortunate in being chosen for slavery.

Over tea one day, he asked Alexander Falconbridge to tell him more about the methods used to secure slaves. Falconbridge gave him a detailed briefing.

"On the arrival of the ships at Bonny (near Calabar, which is a little south of the Bite of Benin) it is customary for them to unbend the sails, strike the yards and topmasts, and begin to build what they denominate a house," Falconbridge said. "The slave ships generally lie a mile below the town, in Bonny river, in seven or eight fathoms of water. Sometimes fifteen ships—English and French—but chiefly English, meet here together.

"After they cast anchor, the captains go on shore to make known their arrival and to inquire into the state of the Trade," Falconbridge continued. "They also invite the kings of Bonny to come on board. (The captains usually make presents (termed *dashes*) which generally consist of pieces of cloth, cotton, chintz, silk handkerchiefs, and other India goods and sometimes brandy and beer.

"The kings of Bonny demand respect. Every ship, on its arrival, is expected to send a present to these gentlemen and to treat them whenever they come on board. Their approach to the ship is announced by blowing through a hollow elephant's tooth.

"After the kings have been on board and have received the usual presents, permission is granted for them to do business with the black traders. When the royal guests leave the ship they are saluted by guns.

"From the time of the arrival of the ships to their departure—usually about three months—scarcely a day passes without some Negroes being purchased and carried on board. The total number taken on board depends on circumstances. In a voyage I once made, our stock of merchandise was exhausted in the purchase of about 380 Negroes, when it was planned to buy 500. The large number of English and French ships then at Bonny had raised the price."

Falconbridge went on to explain how the demand for slaves either raised or lowered their value. Once, when the price was very low, he inquired the reason. One of the black merchants informed him that the low price was due to some people called Quakers who were attempting to abolish the Trade. The informant told Falconbridge that this was a very bad thing, and that the Quakers ought to be reduced to the same state—obliged to dig the ground and plant yams.

"In other words," cut in Wilberforce, "the black traders were unhappy when the Trade slacked off because that meant they had to go to work!"

"Exactly," replied Falconbridge.

"Now tell me more about how the slaves are purchased," said Wilberforce, his pad and pen poised and ready to write.

"After permission has been obtained for breaking trade, as it is termed, the captains go ashore to examine the Negroes that black traders are offering for sale," Falconbridge explained. "The slaves are bought by the black traders at fairs, which are held for that purpose, as much as 200 miles from the seacoast. Many slaves report that they traveled several moons before they reached the place where they were purchased by the black traders. At these fairs, which are held every six weeks or so, several thousand blacks are frequently offered for sale.

"During one of my voyages, the black traders brought down from twelve to fifteen hundred Negroes who had been purchased at one fair. They consisted chiefly of men and boys. From forty to 200 Negroes are generally purchased at a time by each black trader, according to the wealth of the buyer. The slaves range in age from one month to sixty years—and upwards. Sometimes pregnant women are purchased who give birth on the ship.

"There is considerable evidence that most of the Negroes shipped from the coast of Africa have been kidnapped," Falconbridge continued. "I was told by a Negro woman that she was kidnapped on her way home from some neighbors she had been visiting. Although she was big with child she was sold as a slave.

"Frequently those who kidnap others are themselves seized and sold. Although wars among the Africans are said to furnish large numbers of slaves, I never saw any Negroes with recent wounds. And since it was my job as surgeon to examine the slaves when they were purchased, some battle wounds should have been obvious."

Falconbridge paused and wiped some perspiration from his forehead.

"What happens when a captain does not want to buy a certain slave?" asked Wilberforce, peering closely at Falconbridge's face and rubbing his fingers, fatigued from so much writing.

"At New Calabar, in particular, the traders have been known to put them to death. Sometimes when Negroes were refused the traders paddled their canoes under the stern of the vessel and beheaded them in sight of the captain."

Wilberforce verified the information supplied by Falconbridge with the abundant testimonies of others. He began to sift and assemble facts which concerned the Middle Passage. Sometimes he worked until his failing eyes could barely see.

From many witnesses he learned that it was customary to wedge slaves into every available space on the ship. To make certain that every square inch was used, elaborate charts were drawn—and followed.

Captain Knox admitted that the height of the hold in his ship was only five feet ten inches. and that this space was divided in two by a wide shelf on which a second layer of slaves was placed. Thus, the distance between the shelves was a mere two feet and ten inches. He stated that generally his slaves had sufficient room to lie on their sides. but agreed that this was not always the case.

When asked if this was not cruel, he shrugged. Of the 602 slaves on his last voyage only nine had died in the Middle Passage, he said, and that wasn't bad.

Falconbridge came forward with a much worse horror story. The measurements of a 235-ton Liverpool slaver, he declared, were twenty-five feet across at the widest place, and between decks it was ninety-two feet in length. The ship contained four rooms, one of which was for storage. The congestion was so great fifteen slaves died before the ship sailed from the Bonny River. Another 300 died during the Middle Passage. In this instance, the slaves were so crowded many actually had to lie on top of one another!

"They didn't have as much room as a man in his coffin either in length or breadth," Falconbridge observed.

Wilberforce also determined to know how the slaves were branded, fed, and sold. He learned that often as many as three sets of irons were used on each slave. One iron scorched the name of the captain into their flesh, another his trademark, and the third, his arms' symbol. As the slaves screamed in pain and terror during this ordeal, the captain and the trader casually talked about their business and sometimes refreshed themselves with a glass or two of port.

After being branded, the slaves were shackled together two by two. Manacles were placed on their wrists and their ankles. Thus, escape was impossible. In this condition, on most European ships, they were driven to their allotted space in the hold. The Portuguese insisted on baptizing each slave as he was taken on board and providing him with a mat to lie on. An English observer of these refinements was not impressed. He felt it was pure hypocrisy, for the ship he visited was so crowded the men were standing in the holds tied to stakes.

Food on the slavers was fairly standard. It consisted of horse beans boiled to a pulp and covered with "slabber sauce," a mixture of flour, palm oil, red pepper, and water. Accustomed to eating manioc and yams, the slaves hated horse beans and often threw them into each other's faces.

The slaves were fed twice a day and along with each meal were given a half a pint of water. As they ate, they were watched by sailors armed with cat-o'-nine-tails.

Following the morning meal, the slaves were driven to the top deck and forced to dance—jump up and down—to a crude rhythm produced by beating a kettle, drum, or even the use of wind instruments. Some slavers employed bagpipes. As the slaves thumped the decks in their irons, they were scrutinized by armed guards. Those who lacked "enthusiasm" were speeded up by the cat-o'-nine-tails.

Many slaves danced until their ankles were raw and bleeding.

"And how do the slaves respond to all of this?" inquired Wilberforce.

"Many commit suicide," said one.

"How can they do that when they are constantly being watched?"

"The most frequent way is through 'fixed melancholy,'" replied a former surgeon on a slaver.

"Explain it."

"All I can say is that the slaves *will* to die. Guards are alerted to watch for this condition. When a guard notices a slave with a fixed, vacant stare—especially if the slave is squatting on the deck with his head between his knees—he leads him around the deck to get his mind on something else. He may give the slave a dram of rum."

Dr. Wilson, an ex-surgeon on the *Elizabeth*, declared that no one who had it was ever cured. "The symptoms are a lowness of spirits and despondency," he explained. Hence they refuse food. This only increases the symptoms. The stomach afterwards gets weak, the belly aches, fluxes ensue, and they are carried off."

Fixed melancholy was especially prevalent among the Ibo and other tribes that gathered food. Missing their friends and ordered life was too much.

Dr. Ecroide Claxton, surgeon on a ship packed with Ibo which had just completed its voyage, stated that some of the slaves wished to die in the hope that they would get back into their own country. To suppress this idea, the captain cut off the heads of those who had died, and he did so in the presence of the other slaves. Then he said, "Now if you do get back to your own country you will do so without heads!"

Falconbridge reported on typical "sanitary facilities" on a slave ship. "Each of the compartments contains three or four large cone-shaped buckets nearly two feet in diameter at the bottom and only a foot wide at the top and about twenty-eight inches deep. On the way to relieve themselves those who are placed at a distance from the buckets often tumble over their friends because of their shackles. These accidents spark quarrels. Unable to proceed, they ease themselves where they are. This leads to more quarrels."

Often the slaves had to lie in their own filth for days—and even weeks at a time.

Wilberforce learned that once the voyage was completed—they averaged from seven to eight weeks—the ships dropped anchor near the port where they planned to sell the slaves. The slaves were then given extra food to fatten them up. Also, their wounds and diseases were carefully disguised. Yaws, for example, was concealed by a mixture of gunpowder and iron rust.

Occasionally an entire shipload of slaves was purchased by one planter. But the usual method was to turn the healthier slaves over to a dealer who sold them for a fifteen percent commission. Less desirable slaves were sold in a "scramble."

The procedure of a scramble was simple. After confining the crippled or sick slaves to a certain part of the ship or an enclosure on the wharf, the seller announced a bargain price. this price applied to any of the slaves. At a signal, often the firing of a pistol, the buyers barged in to make their selection. Each buyer was given a tag to tie around the slaves he selected.

Since the slaves had no idea what was taking place, many thought they were about to be cooked and eaten. Frequently some died of fright or lost their minds. Occasionally one or two managed to evade the guards and drowned themselves.

Slaves not sold in the scramble were left to die without food or water on the wharfs or were practically given away on speculation. Sometimes a doctor would buy one of these for five or six dollars, hoping he could effect a cure and make some money. Many were sold for a dollar, or even less. The inventory sheet of a wealthy planter in Jamaica listed the value of his slaves. The highest priced one was valued at £330. This was "Jimmy, an accomplished mill carpenter in his prime." The lowest priced one was "Quamina, a good watchman, but with bad legs." He was priced at 6d—ten American cents!

Having been sold, the slave was submitted to a seasoning process. Realizing that their newly purchased slaves came from a different climate, were not accustomed to different diet, and had not worked under the lash, the plantation owners broke the new slaves in with "light work" for several years. During this hardening process—for in reality that is what it was—fully one third of the slaves died.

At the end of a grueling day, a servant opened the library door. "Mr. Wilberforce," he said, "there's a black man at the door who wants to see you. He says that he's an old friend." "Send him in," said Wilberforce, lifting a tired face from the thick book he was reading.

Seconds later, Wilberforce was on his feet. "Socrates!" he half-shouted, seizing both of his visitor's hands in his own. "Oh, it's good to see you!" He looked him over carefully. Then he frowned. "But Socrates, where's your silver collar?"

"That's the reason—"

"Never mind," cut in Wilberforce, throwing up a hand. "No one should speak on an empty stomach—especially an old friend!"

He shook the brass bell for the butler. "Make us some tea and bring plenty of tarts—especially those strawberry ones. And please don't let anyone interrupt us for the next two hours."

"Yes, Mr. Wilberforce," replied the smartly uniformed man. He clicked his heels and vanished into the kitchen.

9
CALICO GUTS

"WHAT HAPPENED to your collar?" asked Wilberforce, peering at the place where it had been.

"After I grew up," said Socrates, "Captain Beef told me that I was too old for his purpose—that he was going to replace me with a boy he had just purchased in Africa. He said he was going to sell me on the steps of the Royal Exchange.

" 'How much do you want?' I asked.

" '£25,' he said. 'I've got to get that much because you ain't no ordinary nigger. You can read and even draw.'

"That seemed like a mountain of money to me. But when I asked him if he'd give me my freedom if I raised it, he nodded. I could hardly believe my ears.

"As I was thinking about where I'd get the money, I remembered Sam Johnson had left an income and some cash to his servant, Francis Barber. I knew Barber had been a slave and so I went to him and he gave me the money to buy my freedom." Socrates withdrew a folded piece of parchment from his coat pocket. "See, here's the document that proves I'm free. Notice, it's signed by Captain John Beef and two witnesses.

"Yes, Mr. Wilberforce, I'm just as free as any white man!"

"Congratulations!" exclaimed Wilberforce. He reached over and pumped his hands again. "That's the best news I've heard in weeks. And now what are you going to do?"

"That's why I came to you. I need advice." Socrates' dark eyes glistened with a fierce new light. "Since I'm free, I could do several things. I could study art. As you know, I love Hogarth. But I made a promise to my mother on the slave ship—and I must keep it. Captain Beef paid only three bottles of rum for both of us, but Mr. Wilberforce, my mother was a very great woman! She was an excellent sculptress. I think I got my talent from her. Mother was also a Christian in her own limited way.

"A man in our village had found a tract in a bottle when he was out fishing. This man couldn't read very well. Still, he managed to read enough of it that several people became Christians. My mother was one of these. I can still see him as he read by the campfire while the people sat around him and listened. He would read the whole tract and then someone would ask him to read it again. Finally the tract was worn out. But by this time the people knew it by heart.

"Mother was always helping people. When a neighbor was sick she'd go over and dig her garden and carry her water. As a matter of fact that's what she was doing when we were kidnapped—"

"And what happened to your father?"

"I-I don't know. He was sharpening a knife when we left. Perhaps he was told that we were kidnapped. Perhaps not. But I think he knows because both his mother and sister were kidnapped years before. . . .

"After they had branded and shackled us we were stored in the ship. The ship remained in the river for two months before sailing."

"Why so long?"

"Because Captain Beef had a hard time getting enough slaves to fill the holds. You see some French and Danish ships had loaded up with slaves just before he came.

"When we finally sailed, Mother became very sick with the flux. She couldn't stand the motion of the ship and she hated the horse beans and slabber sauce. Besides, her hold was jammed with slaves. It was so full none of them could put their shoulders on the floor. And the smell was terrible. In addition, lying on one's right side for days at a time gets pretty wearisome.

"Since I was a little fellow and not likely to jump overboard, Beef removed my shackles and let me visit Mother. Each day she begged me to pray for her, and each day she got worse. Finally she knew she was going to die. I'll never forget that day. She took my hand in both of hers and whispered, 'Son, I'm about to leave you. Before I do, I want you to promise me two things. Promise that you will always pray for Captain Beef. You see, he doesn't really know what he's doing. If he did, he wouldn't do it. And I want you to promise that you'll do all you can to put an end to slavery.' "

He choked on the lump in his throat for a moment. Then he went on. "Mr. Wilberforce, I made that promise. Minutes later Mother was dead. That evening, just as the sun was touching the sea, some big sailors came into the hold and unshackled her. I followed them up the stairs.

"At the deck rail, one man stood on one side and the other man on the other side. They swung her back and forth three times and then heaved her into the sea like a sack of garbage."

"Did anyone put her body in a shroud or say a prayer?" asked Wilberforce, his face pale with horror.

"No, Captain Beef never wrapped anyone in a shroud— not even his own sailors. And as you know, he flogged many of them to death. Beef said that throwing good cloth away was a waste of money."

The butler placed a silver tray of tea on the table. Wilberforce filled the cups and passed the tarts to Socrates. "I'm not hungry," he murmured. "You'll have to eat them yourself." Each emptied his cup in silence.

Then Socrates said, "Mr. Wilberforce, I know what you're trying to do for the slaves. You've chosen a hard task, and you are making many enemies. Just a month ago some slave captains came to see Beef. Since Beef needed a waiter, he summoned me. While they were eating, I overheard some of their talk. One of them said that he had just returned from Jamaica and that while he was there he heard several knots of slaves discussing you.

"This captain said the slaves shouted, 'Wilberforce for Negro! Parliament for Negro! God for Negro!' "

"And what did the captains say?"

"Oh, they said a lot, Mr. Wilberforce. They are all agreed that they're going to fight you in Parliament with every shilling they can raise, and they claim the entire city of Liverpoool is behind them. The owner of Scipio is afraid there'll be a slave uprising in Jamaica because of your work. He says that if there is such an uprising it will finish the abolitionists."

"What are you planning to do?" asked Wilberforce thoughtfully.

"Mr. Wilberforce, I've arranged passage for Jamaica! I'm leaving tomorrow. While I'm there, I'll keep writing to you and telling you what's happening."

"You'll be risking your life!"

"Yes, but so are you, Mr. Wilberforce."

As Socrates stood to go, Wilberforce put £25 in his palm. "You will be a great help," he said. "I'll be praying for you, and I want you to pray for me and the Committee."

At the next meeting of the Committee, a new member was introduced. He was James Stephens—an attorney from the West Indies. "I think he'll be a great help to us," said Wilberforce, "because he knows the law."

"But do you hate slavery?" demanded Clarkson.

"I'll tell you what I think of slavery," said Stephens, his eyes narrowing to slits. "I'd rather be on friendly terms with a man who had strangled my infant son than support an administration guilty of slackness in suppressing the slave trade!"

"Hear! Hear!" shouted several.

"Tell them why you hate slavery so much," prodded Wilberforce.

"I lived in the West Indies for eleven years, and so I

know what it's all about. On my way to St. Christopher, I attended a court session in Barbadoes. Two slaves were being tried. The poor fellows had no adequate defense and when they were sentenced to be burned alive, I could hardly believe what I was hearing. If all members of Parliament knew what I know, there would be no more slavery!"

At the end of the preliminaries, Wilberforce said, "I don't want to alarm anyone, but this may be the last time I can meet with you! My digestive tract isn't working properly. I have no appetite, I have a constant thirst and high temperature, and my eyes are giving up. Right now, I can barely see you. The only reason I'm here is because of determination.

"But even if I'm not with you, the work must go on. It's our sacred duty to abolish slavery! Prime Minister Pitt has promised me that he will work with you, and that he will propose a motion against the Trade in the House. As you know, this is a necessary procedure before the debates can begin."

Wilberforce had been clutching at his stomach. Now he began to sway. "Water! Water! I-I must have water!" he gasped breathing hard. Sharp handed him a glass with a pitcher. After he had emptied two glasses, he continued.

"Right now, I think we should go over our material and get it into the best possible shape for the Privy Council inquiry." He gulped another glass of water. "The opposition has the money to hire the best legal brains in England to stop—or delay—abolition of the Trade. Mr. Clarkson—God bless him!—has not spared himself to assemble statistics. Perhaps he can now show us one of his charts."

Year	No. of vessels	Original crews	Died of original crews	Brought home of original crews
1784-1785	74	2,915	615	1,279
1785-1786	62	2,163	436	944
1786-1787	66	2,136	433	1,073
1787-1788	68	2,422	623	1,114
Total	270	9,636	2,107	4,410

"Mr. Clarkson," said Sharp, "I notice that in the year '84-'85 there were 2,915 members of the crews and 615 of them died. According to these figures, there should be 2,300 left, but you've indicated that only 1279 remained. What happened to the other 1021?"

"I'm glad you asked that," replied Clarkson. "The other 1,021 either jumped ship or were discharged. I have stacks of records showing that sailors are frequently beaten to death, thrown overboard, starved—and shot. Many captains are deliberately mean to their men, especially when they are in West Indian ports. The reason is that if a sailor deserts he does not have to be paid for any part of the voyage. And sometimes that payment can be a tidy sum."

Clarkson shuffled through a pile of papers and selected one near the top. "Here's the story of a captain who had a sailor flogged to death with a cat. The details are too gory to read. . . ." He pulled out another sheet. "This one tells the fate of the cook on the *Alexander*. After he had been flogged until his back was raw from his neck to his hips, his wounds were rubbed with salt and cayenne pepper...

"Ah, and here's another tale related to me by Dr. Falconbridge—a gentleman I've always found to be reliable. The story concerns a boatswain. 'Having complained about the water allowance, one of the officers seized him and beat out several of his teeth. Then one of the pump bolts was fixed in his mouth and kept there by a piece of rope yarn. Unable to spit out the blood that flowed from his gums, he almost choked to death.'"

James Stephens stood up. "I have a question," he said, speaking in the tones of a lawyer. "According to the chart, more than one fifth of all the crews on slaving ships die before the voyage is completed. In addition, there are undoubtedly many deaths among those who desert or are discharged. Now I would like to know how these figures compare to those who die on non-slaving voyages to the West Indies."

"I made a study of that also," replied Clarkson. "Here's what I found. Out of 462 vessels which carried 7,640 seamen only 118 were lost. And that amounts to less than one in sixty-five compared to one in two on the slavers."

"Why the difference?" asked John Barton from the back row.

"Brutality!" answered Clarkson.

"Do you have any tables on the number of slaves who are lost?" asked John Lloyd.

"I do," said Clarkson. "I'll have them for you in just a moment."

"Gentlemen, I'm afraid I'll have to leave you at this point," groaned Wilberforce. "My abdomen seems to be on fire!"

Wilberforce consulted the finest doctors in London. None were hopeful. Dr. Warren remarked to a friend, "That little fellow with the calico guts cannot possibly survive twelve months." Medical opinion was that he was suffering "an entire decay of all vital functions." Next, Wilberforce consulted Dr. Pitcairne.

"I'm going to put you on opium and send you to Bath," said the famous man. "The waters there have helped many."

"But opium?" exclaimed Wilberforce.

"It's perfectly legal," said Pitcairne. "Thousands of people use it—even your good friend Isaac Milner."

Wilberforce still hesitated.

"Have you ever heard of Godfrey's Cordial?"

"Yes, of course. It's a children's tonic."

"Well, there's opium in that," said Dr. Pitcairne. "Your main problem will be to restrict yourself to a moderate dosage."

A few weeks later, Wilberforce paid the £35 postage due on his mail. As he picked it up, he remarked, "I hope the time comes when the sender instead of the receiver has to pay the postage. When it does, I won't get so much mail!"

Among the letters was a long one from Socrates. Delighted, Wilberforce read it first. Socrates wrote that he had settled in Kingston, Jamaica, where he was attending a Baptist Church. Following a page of chitchat, he came to a grim paragraph.

"On Monday morning I was down at the wharf," wrote Socrates. "A ship from Guinea had arrived and the captain was selling his slaves. As I watched the planters examine the women, I was embarrassed. One man in particular was most revolting. I am sure that if he had examined an English mule as I watched him examine the women, the mule would have kicked him fifty feet.

"Having purchased his slaves, this man—he had a full red beard—spat into each one of their faces. Why, I don't know. Perhaps it was to show that he owned them.

"I shall be writing to you again—soon."

Wilberforce filed the letter and then retired to his bedroom. He wanted to think and to pray.

10
PAINFUL COMPROMISE

WILBERFORCE was near death when he reached Bath on April 5. Friends who came to visit were forced to turn their heads to hide their anxiety. But within a week he began to mend. At the end of thirty days he was strong enough to move to Cambridge. Indeed, he rode part of the way on horseback!

He remained for a month at St. John's—his alma mater. Next he moved to a cottage in the lake district. He was now strong enough to renew his correspondence. To John Newton he wrote, "At this moment my cottage overflows with guests."

This was at a time when Wilberforce needed absolute quiet and the old African blasphemer was worried. "He had better take care of his health," he sighed.

Wilberforce was further cheered when he learned that Pitt had invited Sharp to 10 Downing Street on April 21 to brief himself so that he could adequately press the Privy Council inquiry. He was also told that on May 9 Pitt had introduced a motion which bound the House of Commons to consider the Trade early in the next session.

Knowing that he was at the threshold of an almost impossible battle, Wilberforce outlined those things he should do for his physical and spiritual health. He determined to always "be in bed if possible by eleven and be up at five o'clock." Also, he decided to have a "full diet good for me, but a simple one, no sweet, no rich things, no mixtures." He flatly declared that gluttony was "the lowest and most debasing of all gratifications."

Wilberforce was as careful with his spiritual life as he was with his body. He spent time with his Bible and prayer book daily. And whenever he read a prayer, he read it slowly to savor every word and clause. He also felt it his duty to relay his faith to others. When an acquaintance found him visiting with an old friend who was on his deathbed, he asked the man how he was feeling. "As well as I can be with Wilberforce sitting there and telling me that I'm going to hell," replied the dying man.

Wilberforce was still away from London gathering strength when the Privy Council proceedings began. This formidable council of twenty-one members was directed by Lord Hawkesbury—a shrewd and methodical man who was determined to uncover the truth. He solicited reports from everyone concerned with the Trade. He even instructed the ambassador in Warsaw to learn what the economic effects would be if the Polish serfs were freed.

At the beginning of the hearings, the slavers produced witnesses who attempted to prove that all the slaves they purchased were either prisoners of "just wars," or people convicted of serious crime. They also proclaimed that the Middle Passage was a time of "great joy" for all the slaves. Some even described the trip to the West Indies as a "holiday cruise" in which the holds were "redolent with frankincense."

As the sessions grew tense, Clarkson, fully alarmed, went to William Pitt. "Mr. Prime Minister," he said, "I have a star witness by the name of Norris who lives in Liverpool. He has given me material that will utterly demolish the testimony of the opposition.

"Would it be possible for the council to summon him to London?"

"No, the council has no power to force any witness to appear," replied Pitt, his fingers forming a steepled church. "The best thing to do is to write him and invite him to come."

Clarkson wrote to Liverpool—only to learn that Norris was in London. Since no address was given, he immediately began searching for him. No one seemed to know of his whereabouts. In desperation, he called on the bishop of London.

"Yes, I saw Norris only yesterday," said the bishop. "He's here in London to testify in behalf of the Trade in these Privy Council hearings."

"In behalf of the Trade!" exclaimed Clarkson, his eyes wide. "I c-can hardly believe it."

"All I know is what he told me," shrugged the bishop lamely.

Clarkson was so overcome by this betrayal, he nearly stumbled on the steps.

Clarkson's pulse raced as he listened in amazement to Norris as he testified. "The king of Dahomey," said this previous informer, "is an absolute monster. I saw two piles of heads at the gates of his palace. They were stacked on top of each other like cannonballs at an arsenal. And every year when he collects the poll tax from his subjects a thousand persons are put to death."

"How about kidnapping—is there any of that?" asked a member.

"None whatsoever," replied Norris.

Aghast at this barefaced contradiction of what Norris had previously said, Clarkson tried to catch his eye. But each time Norris dropped his head and a tinge of scarlet enveloped his face.

As this type of testimony droned on, Clarkson was heartsick. His main concern was not that he had been betrayed by Norris, but rather that all of the committee's efforts seemed to have been wasted and that thousands of sailors and tens of thousands of slaves would perish as a result.

Several days later, his fears were confirmed by a paragraph in the newspaper:

> The report of the Privy Council will be ready in a few days. After due examination it appears that the major part of the complaints against the Trade are ill-founded. Some regulations, however, are expected to take place which may serve to a certain degree to appease the cause of humanity."

This sickening report was followed by another crunching blow. A pamphlet entitled *Scriptural Researches on*

the Licitness of the Slave Trade, showing its conformity with the principles of Natural and revealed religion, delineated in the sacred writings of the Word of God was circulated among the Privy Council and others in authority who could help the Trade. The document had been written by Raymond Harris, a former Jesuit priest.°
The theme of the work was that since slavery had existed in Old Testament times, it was approved and legal in New Testament times.

"What are we going to do?" asked Clarkson as he faced an emergency session of the committee.

"Norris is making it appear that the Trade is humanitarian," said a Quaker in the front row. "And this pamphlet," he displayed it to the group, "insists that slavery is not only scriptural but holy!" He sighed and adjusted his hat, a large Quaker affair which almost reached his eyes. "We must respond at once, and I think we should answer in two ways: First, we should put out a strong pamphlet that will contradict the one issued by Harris. This will be easy to do, for even a child knows the New Testament does not condone slavery. And our second task is to get trustworthy witnesses."

"Let's pray that God will lead us to the right witnesses," said Clarkson. "Believe me, I really checked on Norris, and yet I was deceived. The slavers are passing out bribes. I was told some captains in Liverpool gave Harris £ 100 for his pamphlet."

James Ramsay agreed to write the pamphlet, and the committee voted to send John Newton's *Thoughts on the*

°It was later discovered that his real name was Don Raymondo Hormaza and that he had been suspended from the priesthood by the bishop of Liverpool.

African Slave Trade to all the members of the Parliament—both in the Upper and Lower Houses.

By extreme good fortune, Clarkson met two Swedish botanists who were on their way home from a six-month inspection trip of the African countries bordering the Senegal River. Having been commissioned by the king of Sweden, they were just the kind of people the committee needed.

"Did you make notes?" asked Clarkson, his heart thumping.

"We most certainly did," replied Dr. Andrew Spaarman, a professor of physics. "We have books full of them."

"And would you be willing to testify to what you have seen before the Privy Council?" Clarkson held his breath.

Spaarman consulted with his companion, C. B. Wadstrom—chief director of a Swedish assay office. "Yes, we will help you," he replied in a thick, Swedish accent.

These two gentlemen insisted that they had eyewitness knowledge that wars were fomented by slavers in order to produce slaves, and that kidnapping was an accepted tool of the Trade. They even told how some Africans invited guests into their houses and then sold them into slavery.

Among those who sent out expeditions to gather slaves was the African king of Barbesin. Both men stoutly claimed that they had seen this done. Since they were men of high character, and neither slavers nor abolitionists, their testimony was believed.

Falconbridge, Newton, and others also gave damaging witness against slavery.

As these inquiries were going on, dozens of petitions

denouncing slavery began to come in. They were sent by Quakers, Dissenters, members of the Established Church, and even by cities. The committee was elated, and then a disastrous compromise was proposed.

Sir William Dolben, M.P. from Oxford, had been shocked by his visit to some slaving ships anchored in the Thames for repairs. He stood up in the House of Commons and related the horrors of the Middle Passage. And later he proposed a bill which would limit the number of slaves that could be packed into the ships. He further suggested that this legislation should be tried "one year."

This move irritated the slaving interests of London and Liverpool and they persuaded Lord Penrhyn and William Ewer, an M.P. for Dorchester, to present petitions against the Dolben bill. Their petitions spoke of "the long existence of the slave trade, the essential benefits the country had derived from it, the encouragement that the legislature held out to individuals to embark their fortunes in it, and the injury that they must necessarily suffer from any sudden measure being taken respecting it."

At this point, Sir William lost his temper. He declared that these petitions were "an insult" to the House. He also challenged the merchants to make the trip themselves—"preferably in irons!"

When Penrhyn restated his case, he was crushed by the oratory of Pitt and Fox.

These things were going on when Wilberforce returned to reenter the struggle. Although his intestinal troubles had been arrested, his eyes were as weak as ever. Alarmed by what was happening, he made an early appointment with Pitt.

"This Dolben bill is a terrible thing!" he stormed.

"What's wrong with it?" asked Pitt.

"Come, you know what's wrong with it! It's just a temporary measure to ease the conscience of Britain. We need legislation that will abolish the entire Trade. And when we get that—and we will with the help of God—we must abolish the complete institution of slavery."

"Your long rest has sharpened your tongue," said Pitt with a chuckle. "Believe me, Wilberforce, I agree with you completely. Still, we must face reality. This bill has been introduced and we must deal with it. Personally, I believe the bill can be a great help." His face was lined with care when he finished.

"How?"

"It can be a beginning—a very tiny beginning—of more important legislation. We will be fortunate, however, to even get it passed. The slavers are doing everything—and I mean everything—in their power to stop it. Even my own Cabinet is divided."

The bill was amended, and then the amendments were amended. In the Upper House alone over one hundred amendments were proposed. At first Dolben wanted the ships to be limited to one man per ton. This formula was argued back and forth for days. The average Liverpool slaver started from Africa with two slaves per ton, and reached the West Indies with 1.9 slaves per ton. A decision was finally reached to limit the ships to five slaves for every three tons for the first 200 tons and one slave per ton after that.

Lord Thurlow, a member of the Cabinet and also Lord Chancellor, did all he could to kill the bill. He picked at the wording, ridiculed the abolitionist members of Parliament, and sought postponement. Thoroughly disgusted with his antics, Pitt called a special Cabinet meeting and warned, "If it fails... the opposers of it and myself cannot continue members of the same government." This threat implied that he would resign. And had this happened, Thurlow's political career would have been ruined.

The bill finally passed. But it did so just in time, for a few minutes after it was signed Parliament was dismissed.

Thurlow was incensed. He dubbed the bill the result of "a five-day fit of philanthropy." The slave captains were even more upset. They said they were "ruined." And some of them threatened to move to France!

Wilberforce was thankful that the bill had passed, even though it was an extremely inadequate one. Clarkson drew pictures of the *Brookes*—a slaver which had transported as many as 609 slaves. The drawings showed it loaded with 450—four less than the law allowed under the Dolben bill of 1788. The sketches showed such crowding it was impossible to see where another four slaves could be wedged in regardless of the zeal of the captain.

Pointing to the drawings, Wilberforce said to Pitt, "The amazing thing is that the best mathematicians cannot find a spot for those extra slaves, and yet the ship has carried as many as 159 extra slaves!" He shook his head. "I blush that I'm an Englishman. Someday people will read about us and they will declare that we were monsters."

"I quite agree," said Pitt. "But as I've said, this law is a beginning. Remember it takes a long time to change the course of history. The Magna Charta didn't happen overnight." He got up, glanced out the window, and tested the door to make certain it was locked. Returning to his chair, he motioned for Wilberforce to move closer.

"I'm afraid I have bad news," he said. "Indeed, the news is so bad you must not repeat it under any circumstance. Promise?"

Wilberforce nodded.

"It's about His Majesty. He has been ill for some time, and I'm afraid—deeply afraid—he has a mental problem."

"What does that mean to our work against the Trade?"

"At this point I'm not sure. But should his Majesty go completely insane we will have problems. As you know, many people do not have confidence in his successor, the Prince of Wales. His character is such that few want him to be the king until it is absolutely necessary. And so, if George III does not recover, we will have to have a regency. This will cause many problems because Fox and the Prince of Wales are close. Remember, it was the Prince who helped Fox win at the polls the last time."

Wilberforce did not sleep well that night. He thought of the vast amount of work he and the committee had put into the work against the Trade. It now seemed that all of these efforts might be swept away by a political storm—a storm over which he had no control. His one comforting thought was that although Pitt and Fox were political enemies, both were convinced abolitionists.

Again he sought comfort from the Bible—and John Newton.

11
A NEW DEMOSTHENES

THE KING'S condition continued to worsen. Soon Pitt felt compelled to write to Lord Carmarthen: "I learned that the King's disorder, which has for some days given us much uneasiness, has within a few hours taken so serious a turn that I think myself obliged to lose no time in appraising your Lordship of it."

On Friday, November 7, one of the King's physicians noted: "Pulse 86. The same alienation of mind."

The Queen became so worried she asked the Archbishop of Canterbury "to issue out public prayers for the poor King, for all the churches."

The next day, November 8, Sir George Baker, the King's physician wrote to Pitt: "The dose of James' powder,° which the King had taken before Mr. Pitt left Windsor, produced a gentle perspiration but no dimunuation of the delirium. . .

On the following day it was rumored that the King was dead! Sir George continued to issue bulletins and Wilberforce followed them with great consternation. To him, the King's health was the single horse hair that held the Damocles' sword over the success of his work. By January 17 there were small signs of recovery. But the doctors were still worried. Sir L. Pepys noted that he found "H.M. very deranged, his looks wild & his conversation turned on the usual incoherent topics." He kept planning ways to escape "and tried to bribe the keepers with promissory notes for various annuities."

Dr. Willis decided the King should take a daily dose of "tartar emetic." And since His Majesty would have none of this, Dr. Willis resorted to strategy. "At one time it comes in whey, at another in asses' milk, sometimes in bread and butter, etc."

Soon the King was on his way to health and a political crisis was averted. A rejoicing England struck medals in honor of His Majesty's recovery and Wilberforce along with the committee worked harder than ever.

"The debates on abolition of the Trade will start on May 12, 1789," said Wilberforce, speaking to the committee. "This means that we must anticipate all the argument the opposition can fling at us and be prepared with rebuttal. I anticipate that the slavers will do all they can to annoy us. We may even be threatened with death. But don't worry, God has called us to this task and He will see us through."

° Eighteenth-century aspirin.

As the crucial date approached, Wilberforce went over his material carefully. He did not write a speech to deliver. Rather, he wrote down statistics and prepared himself. As usual, he decided to speak from the overflow.

But Wilberforce was not the only one whose eyes were on May 12. The West Indian planters also kept it in mind. They had a strong lobby in the House and used it to the utmost. Members of Parliament were stopped and gently told that if the Trade were curtailed Britain would face financial ruin. They also resorted to slander, special gifts, intimidation—and even threats of violence.

Several days before the crucial date, Wilberforce received a letter from Thomas Gisborne, his old friend from Cambridge days. Said Gisborne: "I shall expect to read in the newspapers of your being shot by West Indian planters, barbequed by African merchants, and eaten by Guinea captains; but do not be daunted, for—I will write your epitaph."

Wilberforce was not feeling well when he stepped into the House on that historic May 12. As he made his way toward his customary seat, he could feel the tensions of the hour. His opposition was there in force, and so were his abolitionist friends. He nodded to one, smiled at another, and took his seat.

The chamber of the House of Commons had been formed by remodeling St. Stephen's Chapel, and since the time of Edward VI (1537-1553), the interior had not been changed. The Speaker's chair was on the altar steps, the table where the recording clerks jotted down the proceedings was in the center of what used to be the choir, and the whole building was beautifully paneled.

The original ceiling had been lowered, but it was still thirty feet high. And halfway to the ceiling there were three galleries. The galleries for many years were used only by members. Later, visitors used them as well. The inside dimensions were only fifty-seven feet and six inches by thirty-two feet and ten inches. Thus it was considerably smaller than the living rooms of some of the wealthier members. But today it was packed to the doors.

In the remaining moments before his speech, Wilberforce prayed for guidance. And then it happened. The results of his long studies paraded before him in vivid colors. In his mind's eye he saw the shackled slaves, the bodies being tossed to the sharks, and the discarded slaves left to rot on the wharves in the West Indies.

He also seemed to hear the gouging thuds of the cat-o'-nine-tails as it harrowed the flesh of its victims, the pleas of the slaves whose teeth were knocked loose as their jaws were being forced open with the speculum oris, the curses of the captains, and the groans of the sailors as they were being flogged to death.

The smells, too, were realistic. It seemed that he could smell the burning flesh as the branding irons were applied, and even the stench in the holds where the slaves had been lying in their own filth for hours and perhaps even days at a time.

And then the clock indicated that it was time to speak.

A surge of terror fled up and down his spine as he stood to his feet. A nervous glance toward the front showed Grenville in the Speaker's chair and William Pitt facing Charles Fox across the table. Edmund Burke was also present. The sight of these masters of eloquence thrust frozen fingers into his heart. Again he prayed that God would remove all fear and enable him to present the case of the slaves in the best possible manner.

Taking care to start with a low voice, he began:

"When I consider, sir, the magnitude of the subject which I am to bring before the House—a subject in which the interests not of this country nor of Europe alone, but of the whole world and of posterity are involved—and when I think, at the same time, on the weakness of the advocate who has undertaken this great cause, I cannot but feel terrified at my inadequacy to such a task. . . .

"When I reflect . . . that however averse any honorable gentlemen may be, yet we shall all be of one opinion in the end . . . I take courage. I go forward with a firmer step in the full assurance that my cause will bear me out and that I shall be able to justify, upon the clearest principles . . . the total abolition of the slave trade."

By this time the abolitionists were smiling, the undecided were listening with intense eagerness, and scowls were forming on the faces of those who wanted to keep the Trade.

He then began to thrust deeper.

"Does the King of Barbessia want brandy? He has only to send his troops in the nighttime to burn and desolate a village. The captives will serve as commodities that may be bartered with the British trader. . . . Two towns, formerly hostile, had settled their differences and by intermarriage among their chiefs had pledged themselves to peace. But the trade of slaves was prejudiced . . . and it became, therefore, the policy of our traders to renew hostilities. This policy was soon put into practice. . . .

"The slave trade, in its very nature, is the source of such . . . tragedies. . . ."

At this point, the representatives from Liverpool and Bristol were squirming. But Wilberforce was careful not to antagonize them more than necessary. With great diplomacy, he said: "I must now speak of the transit of slaves to the West Indies. This, I confess, is the most wretched part of the whole subject. So much misery condensed in so little room is more than human imagination ever before conceived.

"I will not accuse the Liverpool merchants. I will show them—nay, I will believe them—to be men of humanity. And I will therefore believe that, if it were not for the multitude of these wretched objects, if it were not for the enormous magnitude and extent of the evil which distracts their attention from individual cases and makes them think generally and therefore less feelingly on the subject, they never would have persisted in the Trade. I verily believe that, if the wretchedness of any one of the many hundred Negroes stowed on each ship could be brought before their view, there is no one among them whose heart would bear it.

"Let anyone imagine to himself six or seven hundred of these wretches, chained two and two, surrounded with every object that is nauseous and disgusting, diseased and struggling under every kind of misery! How can we bear to think of such a scene as this! . . .

" 'Their apartments,' Mr. Norris falsely claims, 'are fitted up as much for their advantage as circumstances will admit. The right ankle of one is indeed connected with the left ankle of another. . . . They have several meals a day—some of their own country provisions with the best sauces of African cookery—and, by way of variety, another meal of pulse, etc. . . . After breakfast they have water to wash themselves, while their apartments are perfumed with frankincense and lime juice. Before dinner they are amused in the manner of their country. The song and the dance are promoted. . . .' "

As Wilberforce spoke, he seemed to grow in stature. His shoulders straightened. His eyes flashed. His chin jutted out. No longer did he seem a five-foot shrimp that walked like a man! Now he appeared like the Fourth Man in Nebuchadnezzar's furnace. But instead of merely walking on the burning coals like those in Daniel's story, he boldly picked up burning embers and flung them at the supporters of the Trade with deadly accuracy.

His voice raised and laced with sarcasm, he continued: "What will the House think when by the concurring testimony of other witnesses the *true* story is laid open? The slaves, who are sometimes described as rejoicing in their captivity, are so wrung with their misery at leaving their country that it is the constant practice to set sail at night. The pulse which Mr. Norris talks of is horsebeans, and the scantiness both of water and provisions was suggested by the very legislature of Jamaica.

"Mr. Norris talks of frankincense and lime juice, when the surgeons tell you the slaves are so stowed that there is not room to tread among them. . . . The song and dance, says Mr. Norris, are promoted. It would have been more fair, perhaps, if he had explained that word 'promoted.' The truth is that for the sake of exercise, these miserable creatures, loaded with chains, oppressed with disease and wretchedness, are forced to dance by the terror of the lash. . . .

"As to their singing, what shall we say when we are told that their songs are songs of lamentation on their departure and that, while they sing them, they are always in tears, insomuch that one captain—more humane, as I should conceive him than the rest—threatened one of the women with a flogging because the mournfulness of her song was too painful for his feelings!

"In order, however, not to trust too much to any sort of description, I will call the attention of the House to one species of evidence which is absolutely infallible. Death, at least, is a sure ground of proof; and the proportion of deaths will not only confirm—it will, if possible, even aggravate our suspicions of their misery in the transit.

"It will be found on an average of all the ships . . . which evidence has been given the Privy Council, that exclusive of those who perish before they sail, not less than 12½ percent perish in the passage. Besides these, the Jamaica report tells you that 4½ percent die on shore before the day of the sale which is only a week or two from the time of landing. One third more die in the 'seasoning,' and this in a country exactly like our own—where they are healthy and happy as some of the evidence would pretend.

"The diseases which they contract on board, the astringent washes which are used to hide their wounds, and the mischievous tricks employed to make them up for sale, are one principal cause of this mortality. Upon the whole there is a mortality of about 50 percent—and this among Negroes who are not bought unless quite healthy at first, unless—as the phrase is with cattle—'they are sound in wind and limb.'"

Wilberforce then went on to describe the terrible mortality among the sailors, and to touch on the anticipated argument that if Britain gave up the Trade it would be to the advantage of France.

Dealing with this, he said: "If the slave Trade be such as I have described it, if in truth it be wicked and impolitic, we cannot wish a greater mischief on France than that she should adopt it. For the sake of France, however, and for the sake of humanity, I trust—nay, I am sure—

she will not. . . . Those who argue thus may argue equally that we may rob, murder, and commit any crime which anyone else would have committed if we did not. . . . Let us therefore lead the way. Let this enlightened country take precedence in this noble cause and we shall soon find that France is not backward to follow, nay, perhaps to accompany our steps. . . ."

At the conclusion of his speech, Wilberforce laid down twelve propositions he had culled from the Privy Council Report. These propositions cut the problem to the bone so that all the members could see at a glance what the main thrust of the abolitionists was all about.

Altogether, Wilberforce had been on his feet three and a half hours. His only discomfort was a sore breastbone!

Lords Penrhyn and Gascoyne, both members from Liverpool, now took the floor to defend the Trade. Each predicted that utter ruin would follow if the Trade was hindered. Penrhyn claimed that British subjects held mortages on West Indian plantations which totaled seventy million pounds. If the Trade were abolished, he said, this money could not be repaid.

Both also claimed that Wilberforce had so misrepresented the truth that not a word he said could be believed. Wilberforce responded to this by saying that as far as he knew he had not misrepresented anything. Further, he challenged them to check his twelve propositions with the Privy Council Report.

Burke, with his usual Irish eloquence, supported Wilberforce. He even claimed that Wilberforce's words "were not . . . excelled by anything to be met with in Demosthenes." Pitt and Fox also supported the abolishment of the Trade. But the opposition was determined to defeat the proposal.

Alderman Newnham said abolition would "render the city of London one scene of bankruptcy and ruin."

Newnham's prediction—given with a straight face—was followed by an even more ridiculous claim. Mr. Molyneux solemnly produced a letter which he said he had received from his agent in Jamaica. This document, he insisted, was a complaint against a Mr. Frazer—a man he paid £50 annually to look after his slaves. The complaint insisted that Frazer had neglected to treat "a Negro that was ill in the hothouse with a sore throat."

The absurdity of the accusation brought a smile to Wilberforce's lips, and had he not been deeply concerned, he would have laughed out loud. The next speaker, however, drained all humorous thoughts from the minds of the abolitionists.

"The House," said Viscount Maitland, his face as solemn as a tomb, "would be surrendering its historic rights if it accepted the testimony of the Privy Council. It is our right to hear that testimony ourselves. . . ."

"You mean we have to go over all that material again, even though it may take days?" demanded an abolitionist member angrily.

"That's right!" insisted the Viscount.

Wilberforce and his friends were aghast. But there was nothing they could do about it. The Trade had come up with a delaying tactic—and won. Moreover, the delay would be a long one. Parliament would not be in session again until the next year.

Thoroughly disgusted, Wilberforce pulled a book of humor from a secret pocket. But even though it was by a favorite author, he could find no humor in it. Thrusting it back into his coat, he strode out of the House and headed for his carriage.

12
DEFEAT

DEFENDERS of the Trade knew they could not damage the reputation of William Wilberforce. His zeal and upright character were far too well known for that. And so they did the next best thing. They launched a smear campaign against James Ramsay—vicar of Teston.

West Indian planters hated Ramsay with passion. He had lived in St. Kitts many years before entering the ministry, and they considered him a traitor. Likewise, they smarted from the influence of his book, *Essays on the Treatment of, and Traffic in Slaves*. Many blamed the current stir against the Trade on him.

The planters spewed sewers of invective. According to them, his West Indian life was one of despicable debauchery.* And being an extremely sensitive man, Ramsay collapsed and died under the assault. On July 21, Wilberforce wrote: "Heard that poor Ramsay died yesterday at ten o'clock. A smile on his face now." His sudden death prompted the slavers to gloat. Writing from St. Kitts, Stephen said: "Mr. Molyneux announced the decease of his public enemy to his natural son in this island in these terms: 'Ramsay is dead—I have killed him.'"

On January 27, Wilberforce suggested to the House that evidence be heard by a Select Committee rather than the entire House. The Trade vigorously opposed this, but with the active support of Fox, Pitt, and Burke, Wilberforce had his way.

The Select Committee was appointed and went to work at once. Until the middle of April, it listened only to evidence supplied by the Trade. And then the slavers made an incredible move. All along, they had promoted delay. Now, they wanted the bill voted on at once! This was done so that the abolitionist side could not be heard.

It was late at night when Wilberforce learned of this strategy. Almost numb with such audacity, he did not hesitate. Pulling on his clothes, he scrambled into his carriage and headed full speed to Downing Street. The Prime Minister was in bed when he knocked.

"That's unbelievable!" exclaimed Pitt, rubbing sleep from his eyes. He thought for a long time. Then he said,

---

*On his return from St. Kitts, James Stephen reported: "I have not heard a crime or a blemish imputed to Mr. Ramsay which had not been refuted afterwards in my presence by some of his most inveterate enemies, better acquainted with the facts."

"You'd better take this information to Fox. He's a Whig and head of the opposition."

Fox was sympathetic and promised to do what he could.

Two days later, Wilberforce approached Pitt. "Fox has informed me," he said, "that the Trade is not pressing for an immediate vote before our evidence is heard. He said that the Trade had informed him that they merely wanted to set a time when the actual vote should be taken. If that is true, we'll have plenty of time to press our side."

Pitt frowned. "I hope that's the truth," he said.

The next day Wilberforce watched with apprehension as Alderman Newnham rose to speak. "I think we've already had enough evidence," he said. "Let's vote at once and put an end to this wretched business."

Wilberforce and Pitt exchanged glances. Then Lord Penrhyn leaped to his feet. In smooth, obviously rehearsed words, he declared that if there was not an immediate decision there might be a slave rebellion on the islands. This was so, he said, because the slaves had a mysterious way of knowing what was going on in Parliament. Such a rebellion, he declared, might mean that hundreds of plantation owners would have their throats cut.

This appeal to fear had an immediate effect. All over the House members began to nod approval. A cake of ice settled in Wilberforce's stomach. It seemed impossible for him to believe what he was hearing. The hair holding the Damocles' sword was about to be cut! Visualizing the plight of the slaves, he closed his eyes and prayed. "Dear God," he groaned, "we need Your intervention—now!"

The House, however, was not to be stampeded. It was promptly decided that it would be unfair to have a vote before the abolitionists were heard. Relieved, Wilberforce scribbled in his diary: "Our opponents, blessed be God, fairly beat."

Soon the abolitionists had the privilege of giving their testimony before the Select Committee. Wilberforce went to each session in order to help and to direct his witnesses. Then in June he had to hurry over to York and make a three-week canvass for the general Parliamentary election which was imminent.

Wilberforce was concerned that he might lose his seat. This was because he had spent so much time on slavery he had neglected his constituents. But he need not have worried. He was returned unopposed. Pitt also kept his seat, and, in addition, his party gained new seats.

With Parliament in recess, Wilberforce concentrated on slavery. He toured Wales with Thomas Babington and then the two settled down in the home of Thomas Gisborne on the fringe of the Needwood Forest. They had with them the Privy Council Report and the evidence they had been accumulating—nearly 1,400 pages in all.

A visitor reported: "Mr. Wilberforce and Mr. Babington have never appeared downstairs since we came, except to take a hasty dinner. . . . The slave trade now occupies them nine hours daily. . . . They talk of sitting up one night in each week. . . . The two friends are beginning to look very ill, but they are in excellent spirits."

Wilberforce, however, was not as well as he seemed. This is indicated by his diary: "Oct. 8: Unwell. Hard work—slave evidence. Oct. 9: Eyes bad. Hard at work. Oct. 11: Slave evidence, and very hard at it with Babington all this week: wherein by God's blessing enabled to preserve a better sense of heavenly things than for some time before."

In November Wilberforce was back in London. Here he continued his study of slavery, his interviewing and checking of witnesses. The diary of November 19 speaks of "plunging at once into a dinner circle of Cabinet ministers."

The Committee was also busy. They condensed the Privy Council Report and mailed it to potential helpers. William Cowper helped by supplying a seven-stanza poem, "The Negro's Complaint." The fourth and sixth stanzas are especially moving.

> Is there, as you sometimes tell us,
>   Is there One who reigns on high?
> Has He bid you buy and sell us
>   Speaking from His throne, the sky?
> Ask Him if your knotted scourges,
>   Matches, blood-extorting screws,
> Are the means that duty urges
>   Agents of His will to use?
>
> By our blood in Afric wasted,
>   Ere our necks received the chain;
> By the miseries, which we tasted
>   Crossing, in your barks, the main;
> By our sufferings, since you bought us
>   To the man-degrading mart,
> All sustain'd by patience, taught us
>   Only by a broken heart.

The committee printed the poem on a fine paper and titled the folder, *A Subject for Conversation at the Teatable*. It was distributed by the thousands—and with great effect. And then the famous Quaker potter, Josiah Wedgwood, produced a beautiful cameo which illustrated an imploring slave in chains. It was titled *Am I Not a Man and a Brother?* He gave five hundred of these to Thomas Clarkson alone and large quantities to others.

The cameos were popular. Some had them inlaid on their snuffboxes, others on bracelets. Many had them attached to pins and wore them in their hair. In a short time they became the rage. Thomas Clarkson was delighted. Later he wrote, "And thus the fashion, which usually confines itself to worthless things, was seen for once in the honorable office of promoting the cause of justice. . . ."

Even while these blessings came, Wilberforce made himself attend almost every session in the House. This was because the Trade was determined to amend the Dolben bill. On days when many members of the House were absent, they made special attempts to introduce amendments. But Wilberforce kept a wary eye on them. Often he was so tired he fell asleep while speakers droned on.

The House of Lords was an ominous power. Thurlow took every opportunity to oppose Wilberforce. Then Pitt had an opportunity to help the cause. Lord Sydney resigned as Home Secretary because he disagreed with the Prime Minister on slavery. Pitt immediately replaced him with William Grenville—a staunch abolitionist. In addition, he persuaded the King to make him a baron. This automatically placed him in the House of Lords, where he could be a check to Thurlow.

Wilberforce smiled grimly at this maneuver. It was one of those subtle, and yet expected moves in British politics.

As he fought fatigue and ill health, Wilberforce spent more and more time in prayer. Again and again he went to John Newton for advice and encouragement. And then he received a letter that lifted his spirits and continued to encourage him the rest of his life. The letter read:

London, February 26, 1791

Dear Sir:
   Unless the divine power has raised you up to be as *Athanasius contra mundum*,° I see not how you can go through your glorious enterprise, in opposing that execrable villainy, which is the scandal of religion, of England, and of human nature. Unless God has raised you up for this very thing, you will be worn out by the opposition of men and devils. But, "if God be for you, who can be against you?" Are all of them stronger than God? O "be not weary in well doing!" Go on, in the name of God and in the power of His might, till even American slavery (the vilest that ever saw the sun) shall vanish away before it.
   Reading this morning a tract, wrote by a poor African, I was particularly struck by that circumstance—that a man who has a black skin, being wronged or outraged by a white man, can have no redress; it being a law, in all our colonies, that the oath of a black man against a white man goes for nothing. What villainy is this!
   That He who has guided you from your youth up, may continue to strengthen you in this and all things, is the prayer of
              Dear Sir,
                Your affectionate servant,
                J. Wesley

Four days after writing this letter, Wesley was dead.

As the date for the debates on the Trade in 1791 approached, Wilberforce and the committee intensified

---

°Athanasius against the world.

their work. They checked evidence, had detailed conferences with those they believed would stand with them, and made certain the witnesses were reliable—and available. The betrayal by Norris was still ground glass in their eyes. They could not take chances!

Even before this period Thomas Clarkson has gone to Paris to try to persuade the French to abolish the Trade in their empire. If this could be done, it would flatten the argument that France would take advantage of the Trade should Britain vote for abolition.

In the beginning, Clarkson was flushed with apparent success. He met Comte de Mirabeau—a leading French abolitionist. "You are just the man I need," exclaimed the Frenchman. "I have been preparing a speech on slavery for the National Assembly. Now I need eyewitness material." Delighted, Clarkson bombarded him with current information. For an entire month he mailed him daily a sixteen to twenty-page letter.

Clarkson also employed a cabinet maker to build a yard-long model of the slave ship *Brookes* for Mirabeau's dining room. The ship was complete with painted-in figures of the slaves. Soon he was having conferences with such leading Frenchmen as Lafayette and Jacques Necker, the Minister of Finance.

"His Majesty Louis XVI would like to have two copies of your book, *Essay on the Impolicy of the Slave Trade*," said Necker.

Highly gratified, Clarkson asked if he could present the King with a model of the slave ship.

Necker was thoughtful. "I don't think you should do that," he said, his chin cupped between his thumb and forefinger. "It is—should I say—rather dramatic. The shock might upset His Majesty!"

Clarkson was still in France when the palace of Versailles was invaded by the mob and Louis XVI, along with his queen, Marie Antoinette, were seized and escorted as "prisoners of the people" to the Tuileries in Paris.

The French Revolution, predicted by Pitt, had begun.

As fighting broke out in France, slave uprisings were launched in the French West Indian colony of Santo Domingo. Within a few months 100,000 slaves had pillaged 1,000 plantations and killed 2,000 whites. Also, 1,200 white families were reduced to poverty.

Wilberforce was heartsick. He did not believe in violence, and he feared the rebellion would defeat his bill. Fortunately for his cause, the worst of the insurrection was still ahead. Still, he knew what had happened could have a disastrous effect on the forthcoming vote in the House.

As the day for the crucial test approached, Wilberforce wrote in his diary: "May I look to Him for wisdom and strength and the power of persuasion . . . and ascribe to Him all the praise if I succeed, and if I fail, say from the heart, 'Thy will be done.' "

From the beginning of the debate, it was clear the abolitionists were the losers. Mr. Drake, standing for the Trade, summed up the situation neatly: "The leaders, it is true, are for abolition. But the minor orators, the dwarfs, the pygmies will, I trust, this day carry the question before them. The property of the West Indies is at stake. . . ."

The vote was not taken until three-thirty on the morning of April 20. Wilberforce was overwhelmingly crushed. To some, it seemed his career was completely finished—that he would be forced into retirement. The final tally showed that he had lost by a vote of 163 to 88.

Believers in the Trade gloated and the slave captains polished their gold buttons with new confidence. A rash of cartoons vilifying Wilberforce appeared in the newspapers. The event provided an opportunity for Boswell to be revenged over the way he had been ridiculed at the abolitionist dinner.

Indulging himself, Boswell wrote:

> *Go, W— with narrow skull,*
> *Go home and preach away at Hull.*
> *No longer in the Senate cackle*
> *In strains that suit the tabernacle;*
> *I hate your little wittling sneer,*
> *Your pert and self-sufficient leer.*
> *Mischief to trade sits on your lip,*
> *Insects will gnaw the noblest ship.*
> *Go, W— begone, for shame,*
> *Thou dwarf with big resounding name.*

13
DEFEATED AGAIN

THE EARLY RAYS of the sun were feeling their way through the streets as Wilberforce stepped from the House. He and the committee had fought hard—and lost. But although his face was lined and he was bone-weary, he was not defeated. There would be another day!

Soon he was busy again. Early in 1792 he planned the outline of a new strategy. "The best course," he wrote to a friend, "will be to endeavor to excite the flame as much as possible in a secret way, but not to allow it more than to smoulder until after I have given notice of my intention of bringing the subject forward. This must be the signal for the fire's bursting forth."

With Wilberforce's help, the committee in London

created other committees throughout the country. These committees fed exciting stories to the newspapers, arranged for rallies, and worked with churches. They also encouraged the writing of petitions, but warned the people to hold them until the right time. Slavery was becoming a dramatic issue and the committees were effective.

When a famous actor was hissed off a Liverpool stage because he was intoxicated, he whirled on the audience and sneered that he had not come to be insulted by a pack of men every brick in whose detestable town was cemented by the blood of a Negro. The obvious truth in the insult was so apparent the audience was decent enough to cheer. Yes, public opinion was changing!

But even as Wilberforce worked, the Trade did likewise. And now they had a new theme: the massacres in Santo Domingo. They dramatized the number killed and the often dreadful way in which they had been killed. "And this will happen to us if we're not careful," they claimed.

Another weapon they used concerned the French Revolution, which was darkening many a street with blood. The Trade now claimed that Wilberforce, without understanding what was happening, was being used by the French revolutionists to further their cause. And this claim was further strengthened when the Convention made Wilberforce an honorary citizen of France!

Deeply alarmed, Wilberforce consulted Edmund Burke. "Why don't you join the committee which is providing relief for fleeing French clergymen?" suggested the man from Ireland. Wilberforce complied, but whatever good this may have done was counteracted by Clarkson, who could not resist praising the revolution.

The Trade kept gaining power. Wilberforce was so shaken he wrote: "I am pressed on all hands . . . to defer my motion until next year." And among those who were frightened because of Santo Domingo was Pitt himself. Indeed, the Prime Minister wanted him to put off his motion until the next year.

That Pitt would waver, alarmed Wilberforce. He wrote to Babington: "Do not be afraid lest I should give ground. . . . This is a matter wherein all personal . . . attachments must be as dust in the balance."

Pitt's hesitation did not last. Soon Wilberforce had him back in the fold as enthusiastic as ever. That accomplished, Wilberforce indicated to the House that he would soon propose a motion to abolish the Trade.

As planned, the committee chairmen now sent their petitions to Parliament. For several days, each mail brought in new ones. Altogether, 312 came from England and Wales, while another 187 arrived from Scotland. And then the abolitionists got an unexpected boost. On March 16, King Christian VII of Denmark signed an edict which decreed that "with the beginning of the year 1803, all traffic in the slave trade by our subjects shall cease."

Wilberforce and the committee were delirious with joy.

Finally the time came when Wilberforce stood again in the House and spoke against the Trade. This time his subject was not fresh, for he had gone over much of his material in his previous three-and-a-half-hour speech. But he had some new material, and he used it effectively. Some of his sentences cut like a surgeon's knife. Once he exclaimed: "Europeans are hovering round the coast like vultures, and like vultures, they feed on blood."

He also told them a verified story about six British slave ships that had anchored just off the coast of Calabar. When the captains learned that the price of slaves had been raised and the traders refused to lower it, they opened fire with sixty-six cannon. "Not a shot was fired in reply, but the inhabitants could be seen running in all directions like ants in a broken nest. The bombardment was continued for three hours and resumed again in the evening. After twenty people were killed and many injured, the natives consented to sell their slaves at any price the captains fixed. . . ."

All at once several angry voices began to shout, "Name! Name!" Wilberforce hesitated. He did not want to anger the Trade unnecessarily. As he waited, he glanced at Pitt. The Prime Minister's face was ashen, and so was the face of Charles Fox. Still he hesitated. But again, a voice cried, "Name! Name!"

The tension in the House increased. He could not wait any longer and so he decided on compromise. He would name the ships, but not the captains! With his heart throbbing like an African village drum, Wilberforce said, "The ship's names were *Thomas, Recovery,* and *Anatree* of Bristol." There was some confusion when he named the third ship and the reporters were not certain that they had recorded it correctly. He went on. "The *Betsy* and *Thomas* are from Liverpool." The sixth ship was the *Wasp* and he did not name her port. There were two ships named *Thomas.*

The story along with the naming of the ships made a deep impression.

Wilberforce cringed as he was followed by defenders of the Trade. He hoped he had not done the wrong thing. The defenders, however, had nothing new to say.

They dramatized the horrors of Santo Domingo and insisted that financial disaster would fall on the nation if the Trade were stopped. But Wilberforce noticed with some satisfaction that they were not as blatant as they had been. Perhaps the opposition was softening!

Henry Dundas was now on his feet. His theme was that although he was for complete abolition, he felt it was better to do this gradually. Perhaps the House could regulate the Trade.

To Fox, the word "regulation" was like a flame to a dry grass roof. His lips curled as he denounced the idea. He said it reminded him of a passage in Middleton's *Life of Cicero* in which the author said, "To break open a man's house and kill him, his wife, and his family in the night is certainly a heinous crime and deserving of death; *but even this may be done in moderation.*"

Wilberforce squinted at the clock anxiously. Pitt had promised to speak for abolition. Indeed, he had asked Wilberforce to suggest a theme; and when he had suggested that he speak on the civilization of Africa, the Prime Minister had nodded approval. But now it was already after three o'clock in the morning! Would Pitt really speak, or would he waver again? Or, perhaps—and the thought chased chills down his spine—the session would adjourn without a vote. He gazed up into the gallery and noticed several Quaker members of the committee. Their faces seemed as drab as the hats on their heads. They were obviously discouraged.

Wilberforce dropped his eyes and prayed.

The argument over regulation snail-paced along. Dundas insisted that regulation was the answer. It would take much of the horror out of the Middle Passage; it would cause the planters to improve living conditions for their slaves and thus encourage them to have more children. And in time, children born to slaves, could be freed. A gradual program, he insisted, would save the West Indies from bankruptcy.

As the debate sagged and twisted and moved back and forth, the clock ticked on. Members were getting tired. Some forgot to cover their mouths when they yawned. Others were asleep or nearly so. And then when it seemed that neither side would yield, Fox, seeking to bring matters to a head, moved that the word "gradually" be inserted in Wilberforce's motion. This turn shook the sleep out of many an eye.

Wilberforce groaned. Perhaps he would have to settle for another sickening compromise like the Dolben bill! He looked at the clock again. Its hands were moving on. Were they going to snip the hair that held the Damocles' sword? In an hour it would be daylight! Despair gnawed at his heart.

And then William Pitt faced the House. Light from the flickering lamps on the wall lit up his face and spread over his lean cheeks and auburn hair. There was a rustling sound of movement as sleepy members straightened up in their seats. This was followed by a long silence as the Prime Minister studied his audience.

"Mr. Speaker," he began, his voice just loud enough to be heard by everyone, "at this hour of the morning, I am afraid, sir, I am too much exhausted to enter so fully into the subject as I could wish; but if my bodily strength is in any degree equal to the task, I feel so strongly the magnitude of this question that I am extremely earnest to deliver my sentiments."

Wilberforce listened and prayed. Perhaps God would give Pitt the strength to turn the tide! Long columns of slaves, walking two by two in their chains, came before his eyes. He hoped that Pitt would neither compromise nor weaken.

"Why ought the slave trade to be abolished? Because it is an incurable injustice! How much stronger, then, is the argument for immediate rather than gradual abolition!" Pitt's voice now had a touch of thunder in it. "By allowing it to continue for even one hour, do not my right honorable friends weaken—do not they desert their own argument of its injustice? If on the ground of injustice it ought to be abolished at last, why ought it not now? Why is injustice to be suffered to remain for a single hour?"

By this time Wilberforce felt his heart speeding up, and a glance at the gallery showed that the Quakers were leaning forward with keen anticipation. God was answering prayer!

"Think of eighty thousand persons carried away out of their country by we know not what means; for crimes imputed, for light or inconsiderable faults, for debt perhaps, for the crime of witchcraft, or a thousand other weak and scandalous pretexts. Besides all the fraud and kidnapping, consider the villainies and perfidy by which the slave trade is supplied. Reflect on these eighty thousand persons thus annually taken off! There is something in the horror of it that surpasses all the bounds of the imagination."

Continuing with this reasoning, Pitt spoke of the enormity of the evil of slavery and applied it directly to Britain. "Thus, sir, has the perversion of British commerce carried misery instead of happiness to one whole quarter of the globe," he continued. "False to the very principles of trade, misguided by our policy, and unmindful of our duty, what astonishing—I had almost said what irreparable—mischief have we wrought upon that continent! How shall we hope to obtain forgiveness from heaven for those enormous evils we have committed? Shall we, then, delay to repair these injuries and to begin again justice in Africa? Shall we not count the days and the hours that are suffered to intervene and to delay the accomplishment of such a work?"

Pitt's ire had been raised. He was angry with those who argued that Britain should not abolish the Trade because France might take advantage. He stabbed his knife into this problem again and again and each time he twisted it with a vengeance. "How, sir, is this enormous evil ever to be eradicated if every nation is thus to wait until the concurrence of all the world shall have been obtained? Let me remark, too, that there is no nation in Europe that has plunged so deeply into this guilt as Britain."

Those were strong words and defenders of the Trade winced and passed notes to one another. Pitt knew he was making enemies. But he didn't care. However, toward the end he changed his tactics. Subtly, Pitt attempted to make the members see the problem from the slave's point of view.

"There was a time, sir, when even human sacrifices are said to have been offered on this island," he reminded them. "But I would especially observe on this day that the very practice of slave trade prevailed among us. Slaves, as we may read in *Henry's History of Great Britain*, were formerly an established article in our exports. 'Great numbers,' he says, 'were exported like cattle from the British coast, and were seen to be exposed for sale in the Roman market.' It does not distinctly appear by what means they were procured. This historian tells us that 'witchcraft and debt were probably some of the chief sources of British slaves, that prisoners taken in war were added to the number, and there might have been among them some unfortunate gamesters who after having lost all their goods, at length staked themselves, their wives, and their children.' "

As Pitt began to conclude, he was seized with a new inspiration, and at the same time the early morning sun began to shine through the window and bathe his face with light. Wilberforce never forgot his last words. To him, they seemed only inferior to Scripture itself.

"If we listen to the voice of reason and duty," said Pitt, "and pursue this day the line of conduct which they prescribe, some of us may live to see the reverse of that picture. . . . We may live to behold the natives of Africa engaged in the calm occupations of industry. . . . We may behold the beams of science and philosophy breaking in on their land. . . .

"It is my view, sir, as an atonement for our long and cruel injustice toward Africa, that the measure proposed by my honorable friend most forcibly recommends itself to my mind. . . . I shall vote, sir, against the amendment; and I shall also oppose to the utmost every proposition which in any way may tend either to prevent or even to postpone for an hour the total abolition of the slave trade."

Wilberforce sat on the edge of his seat as the vote was taken. Alas, he was disappointed. The amended motion—"That the slave trade ought to be *gradually* abolished"—was carried by a vote of 230 to 85. It was all he could do to keep from weeping! Still, abolition was closer than it had been, and for this he thanked God.

As the weary members stumbled out of the House on

their way to breakfast, Wilberforce seized Pitt's hand in both of his. "We failed," he said, forcing the words beyond the lump in his throat. "But we will try again and again and again. The spider whose web is destroyed will weary before I will weary. God has assured me of final success. I will never give up. Never! Never! Never! The compromise of today condemned no less than one hundred thousand either to death or a life of unspeakable misery!"

While standing at a curb, Wilberforce placed both hands on Pitt's shoulders and turned him so that they were facing one another. Lowering his voice, he asked, "Do you remember when we had refreshments together at the Windsor coffeehouse in Charing Cross?"

"How could I forget it?" asked Pitt, brightening. "It was 3:00 a.m. and we were both full of ambition."

"Yes, and you assured me that you were going to become the Chancellor of the Exchequer, and then Prime Minister. Remember?"

"Of course."

"And do you remember that I told you that when you did a certain thing I would shake your hand?"

"Yes, I remember."

"Well, the time has come to fulfill that promise. Mr. Prime Minister, your speech this morning was greater than any of the speeches your father ever delivered— even in his prime." He grasped Pitt's hand and shook it again. "You were beyond yourself!"

"Ah, but you see, Wilberforce, I had a cause!"

"Yes, and that is the secret of any success. A person must have a cause."

14
DELAYING TACTICS

DURING THE final week of April, the House debated the terms of gradual abolition.

Dundas suggested that the new law should prohibit the exportation of males over twenty years of age and of females over sixteen. Further, he insisted that only ships previously used in the Trade could be employed and that no new countries be added to the list of customers.

To increase the number of slaves in the West Indies, he suggested that the custom duty on girls be less than on boys. This provision, he believed, would increase the birth of slaves and thus balance the loss caused by the new law.

When was this to take effect? Hoping to outdo

Denmark, several Members of Parliament proposed January 1, 1800. Wellesley suggested 1793 and rubbed salt into the proposal with a pinch of sarcasm. "We cannot modify injustice," he said. "Some think we should be unjust for ten years; others think it is enough to be unjust for five years; others . . . that the present century should continue in disgrace."

Wilberforce, Pitt, and Fox insisted that the law be applied at once, but they were outnumbered. The final date selected by a vote of 151 to 132 was 1796.

Wilberforce was pleased, but he was not satisfied. He wrote, "On the whole this is more than I expected two months ago." The would-be law, however, was not complete. The number of slaves that could be exported as the cut-off date for the Trade approached had not been determined.

Wilberforce was still wary. He knew that even after the bill was through the House of Commons, it faced a most formidable obstacle—the House of Lords! And the Upper House was almost a stone wall. Lord Thurlow, still a bitter enemy of Pitt, and an upholder of the Trade, was presiding. Even worse, King George, once a mild friend of abolition, was now a dedicated defender of slavery. His mind had been changed by the massacres in Santo Domingo.

On top of these problems was the grim fact that many of the Lords owned property in the West Indies and a curtailment of slavery was bound to thin their pocketbooks. Wilberforce felt like Moses when he faced the Red Sea and the chariots of Pharaoh were pressing in from behind. But, like Moses, Wilberforce believed in miracles.

Toward the beginning of the debate, the Duke of

Clarence,° made his maiden speech. "I have been an attentive observer of the state of the Negroes," he declared. "I have no doubt but that I could bring forward proofs to convince your lordships that their state is far from being miserable. On the contrary, when the various ranks of society are considered, they are comparatively in a state of happiness." He then added a sting to his argument. "An implicit obedience to the House of Commons, much as I respect the House, would make the House of Peers useless, and thus the natural . . . balance in the constitution would be endangered."

This was the opening statement for delay. And now, just as the House of Commons had repudiated the report prepared by the Privy Council, the House of Lords likewise repudiated the report accepted by the House of Commons!

The House of Commons had at least agreed that the evidence could be heard by the Select Committee. Not so in the House of Lords. The distinguished Lords insisted that the whole House act as the committee. This, of course, was a tactic to stretch the delay to the extreme limit. Even so, Lord Chancellor Thurlow had the blatant nerve to insist that this would not cause delay.

Wilberforce ground his teeth and prayed for courage to continue.

By June 5 only a few witnesses had been heard, for the Upper House was busy with other things. Then, since the session would be closed in ten days anyway, the leadership decided to postpone the hearings until the next session.

°Son of King George III and brother of King George IV. He later became King William IV. Because of his persistent way of ignoring his advisers, he was often dubbed "Silly Billy."

Exasperated, Wilberforce got out John Wesley's letter and reread it. He smiled grimly as he read: "Unless God has raised you up for this very thing, you will be worn out by the opposition of men and devils. But, 'if God be for you, who can be against you?'" Yes, the old man knew what he was writing about! Wilberforce wiped his eyes and straightened his shoulders. He felt he was ready for the battles ahead. Fortunately for himself and the slaves, he had no idea of the intensity of the battles ahead, nor the severity of the struggle.

The French Revolution was entering its most dramatic stage—the Reign of Terror. Joseph Guillotin's newly invented beheading device had been set up in the Place de la Concord. The sound of the dreaded two-wheeled carts—the *tumbrels*—could be heard bouncing almost daily over the cobbled streets while transporting victims to the ever-hungry machine.

Wilberforce shuddered as he read the headlines. Louis XVI, the king with the immense boots, lost his head to the greedy blade on January 21, 1793. Marie Antoinette was hauled to the notorious place on October 16 of the same year. Wilberforce could not forget her tinkling voice and the way she had teased him at Fountainebleau. Now he groaned as he read the story. The scene was as clear to him as if it had taken place in front of his own house.

While the Queen was directed toward the bloody steps leading up to the guillotine, she was momentarily blinded by a strand of hair the wind had blown in front of her eyes. Unable to see, she groped her way up the steps. Halfway up, she accidentally stepped on someone's foot. "Oh, pardon," she exclaimed. Another breath of wind now cleared her vision.

Moments later, with shoulders back and face firm, she knelt before the machine which had taken her husband's life. While she awaited entrance into eternity, the Parisian housewives paused with their knitting. Some even yawned. The bloody event had helped them through another boring day.

Wilberforce had rejoiced when the Bastille—the French political prison—fell in 1789. He also rejoiced when the key to the 400-year-old fortress was sent to George Washington. But he utterly deplored the bloodshed of the occasion and the slaughter that followed. He agreed with the ideals of the rights of man and liberty and equality for all. But he felt the proper way to attain these goals was through democratic processes—not war, firing squads, and guillotines.

Thoroughly shaken by the events across the channel, Wilberforce considered asking the Archbishop of Canterbury to announce a national day of prayer. Already a group of 10,000 Englishmen had paraded through the streets of Sheffield flaunting the French tricolor and he was alarmed.

As England quivered on the brink of revolution, Wilberforce and thousands like him prayed.°

Supporters of the Trade were quick to take advantage of the unrest. Expecting to smash the abolitionists with one blow, the Earl of Abingdon slashed out at Wilberforce in the House of Lords. Standing in his robes, he showed his contempt for the French by calling them "monsters in human shape" and referring to them as

---

°Many historians believe that it was only the Wesleyan revival movement that kept the French Revolution from spreading to England.

"wolves and monkeys." He summed this contempt by saying that it would be better to live as toads on the fumes of a dunghill than to endure the aims and beliefs of the French revolutionists.

These strong statements out of the way, he sought to associate Wilberforce with the leaders of the French Revolution. "And what does abolition of the slave trade mean more or less than liberty and equality?" he demanded. "And what is liberty and equality and . . . the rights of man but the foolish fundamental principles of this new philosophy." Following this, he sneered at the petitions. "What is the ground for them?" he asked. "Humanity! But humanity is no ground for petitioning. Humanity is a private feeling and not a public principle to act upon. *It is a case of conscience, not constitutional right.*" He now insisted that the petitions were illegal "and being illegal, ought not to have been received."

He climaxed his attack by moving that the vote on the bill be postponed for five months.

His motion was seconded by the Duke of Clarence. After thoroughly denouncing James Ramsay, even though he was already dead, he declared that all abolitionists were either fanatics or hypocrites. He included Wilberforce in this class.

Not a single witness was examined in the Upper House until May 6. And after this, only seven were examined before the close of the session. The tactic of delay had worked—and was continuing to work. British slavers were still plowing through the Middle Passage. The sharks were still prospering as they followed the ships. And the branding irons were still scorching human flesh.

As the Earl of Abingdon had planned, the abolitionists had been dealt a mortal blow. In the winter of 1793 the committee had enough life left in them to send Clarkson on another trip to gather evidence. But they were discouraged.

The Committee only had a few meetings in 1794. And during the next three years they only met twice a year. After 1797, they did not meet again until 1804. During this period Clarkson had a nervous breakdown. Since Clarkson had given the best years of his life to the movement, Wilberforce helped raise enough money for him to live in modest comfort the rest of his life.

The slavers gloated as they watched the abolitionists fall one after the other. But all of them knew their business was in constant jeopardy as long as Wilberforce remained alive, and so they turned their attention to him. They arranged for him to be challenged to a duel. They published venomous articles about him. They started whispering campaigns. Indeed, they even attempted to kill him.

Wilberforce ignored them. At the time of his conversion, he had decided to trust himself to God. Whenever he was discouraged, a glance at his spiritual compass renewed his strength.

15
DISCOURAGEMENT

AFTER WILBERFORCE'S conversion, John Newton suggested that he make friends with Henry Thornton. This turned out to be excellent advice and proved that Newton had keen insight.

Like Wilberforce, Thornton was an ardent evangelical—and rich, having inherited a banking business from his father. He was also a member of Parliament. His grandfather, a director of the Bank of England, had purchased a large estate just south of Clapham Common on the outskirts of London.

After his father's death, Henry built a large Queen Anne house on the west side of the common. Eventually he added two wings to this house until it had no less than thirty-four bedrooms! His purpose was to establish a center for evangelical Christians.

Wilberforce felt close to Henry Thornton and lived with him at Clapham for four years. "On the whole I am in hopes some good may come out of our Clapham system," Thornton said. "Mr. Wilberforce is a candle that should not be hid under a bushel. The influence of his conversion is great and striking." Other evangelicals who moved to the area included the abolitionist, Granville Sharp; James Stephen, another abolitionist; Zachary Macaulay; Charles Grant, a former high official in India; and James Eliot, Pitt's brother-in-law. Later, Lord Teignmouth, who followed Lord Cornwallis as viceroy of India, also moved to Clapham.

William Pitt designed a large oval library for Thornton's house. To prove that the evangelicals who lived at Clapham were nonpartisan, busts of both Pitt and Fox were given places of honor! The Clapham sect, as outsiders called them, built a chapel and employed John Venn as their pastor.

The members of the group wandered in and out of one another's houses, often shared the main garden, and were dedicated to philanthropy. They supported missionaries, a Bible society, and worked for abolition. Members of the groups were so fond of one another, they intermarried. In addition to those who lived at Clapham, there were many distinguished honorary members, including Thomas Babington, Isaac Milner, and Hannah More.

When unable to bear the pressures of London, especially in times of defeat, Wilberforce would stay at Clapham for spiritual renewal. As members of Parliament and with large financial resources and complete dedication to the work of improving the world, the Claphamites were a considerable force. But they were also independent. Although he had been elected to Parliament eight times, Henry Thornton did not go out of his way to cultivate his constituents. He liked to say, "I would rather have a shake of the hand of good old John Newton than the cheers of all that foolish mob, who praise one, they don't know why."

As the bill for gradual abolition dragged on in the House of Lords (the slavers saw to it that there was seldom time to listen to the witnesses), Wilberforce sponsored another bill. This one was to abolish the Trade with foreign countries. It failed on the third reading. War had erupted between England and France on February 1, 1793, and Parliament was more concerned with the war than with the abolition of the Trade.

Wilberforce hated the war. He was convinced that if Pitt had negotiated and made compromises, it could have been avoided. Disturbed, he parted ways with Pitt, and this broke his heart—and made him unpopular. One M.P. referred to him as a "wicked little fanatical imp." He was snubbed by the King. And even Clarkson abused him, declaring that he hadn't worked hard enough to have his brother made a captain in the navy.

Friends urged Wilberforce to drop the subject. But after prayer he was convinced that he should continue. Ten days before Christmas in 1795 he announced to the House that since the Trade, according to the Gradual Abolition Bill, was to end in three weeks—January 1, 1796—he planned to bring forward another bill.

Wilberforce proposed the new legislation on February 18. In his remarks he said: "There is something a little provoking in the dry calm way in which gentlemen are apt to speak of the sufferings of others. The question suspended! Is the desolation of wretched Africa suspended? Are all of the complicated miseries of this atrocious trade . . . is the work of death suspended? No, sir, I will not delay this motion, and I will call upon the House not to insult the forbearance of heaven by delaying this tardy act of justice."

When the defenders of slavery declared that the slaves were well clothed, well housed, and well sheltered, Wilberforce lost his patience. "What!" he exclaimed, "are these the only claims of a rational being? . . . So far from thanking the honorable gentleman for the feeding, clothing, and lodging of which he boasts, I protest against the way in which he has mentioned them, as degrading men to the level of the brutes, and insulting all the qualities of our common nature."

Wilberforce's heart fluttered with hope when a motion to close the debate was defeated by twenty-six votes. Since only a few members were present on March 3, the opposition moved for the second reading of the bill. Alarmed, Wilberforce left his supper, seized the floor in the House, and kept speaking until enough abolitionists could be rounded up to win the motion. It was a time of acute anxiety as he watched the abolitionists come trooping in. But he won. Now if only the bill could pass on its third reading! . . .

Alas, he was disappointed. A comic opera, *The Two Hunchbacks*, seemed to have a special attraction for the abolitionists. Instead of being in the House, they were at the theater. The motion lost by a vote of 74 to 70! Wilberforce was disgusted. Since his conversion, he had despised all theatrical performances. Now he had another reason to hate them.

"I am permanently hurt," he lamented. His health, also, sharply declined. He ran a high fever and his intestines seemed to be on fire. Once again he remembered his doctor had said that he had "calico guts."

Nearly shattered spiritually and physically, Wilberforce fled to John Newton.

"I'm not giving up," said Wilberforce with determination from his customary seat in the study. "But my heart is about to burst and I must speak to you."

"That's why I'm here," replied the former slave captain, a broad smile on his face.

"The battle is almost too much for me," confessed Wilberforce. He tried to ignore the huskiness in his voice. "Ours is a Christian nation. We have great cathedrals. We boast of our churches, of Magna Charta, and even of freedom of speech. Our King is a pious man. He is known for his strong Christian faith. And yet His Majesty opposes me and is for the Trade! Why?"

"I-I don't know everything," shrugged Newton. He touched his powdered wig and picked up a set of thumbscrews, which he had been using for a paperweight. "But I am absolutely certain about one thing . . . it takes God a terribly long time to get the simplest truth through our thick skulls!" He bit his lip and closed his eyes. When he opened them there were tears on his cheeks. "Did you ever hear the hymn which begins, 'How sweet the name of Jesus sounds to a sinner's ear!'?"

"Of course! It's one of my favorites."

"Well, I wrote that hymn when I was the captain of a slaver! At the time, my ship was anchored just outside the harbor and we were loading slaves." He bowed his head as he fought his emotions. "I can still see those wretches as they were pushed on board. Some were so frightened they trembled from head to toe. But their misery didn't bother me. As a matter of fact, I could smell the filth and hear their groans as I wrote the hymn."

"Oh, but at the time you weren't converted!"

Newton hung his head and wiped his eyes. "I'm afraid you are mistaken. I had been converted. I was also bubbling with Christian zeal. I read the Bible daily and led regular public worship. The crew even called me a fanatic."

"Surely you had a twinge of conscience!" said Wilberforce, squinting at his friend with unbelief.

"Not a bit. You see I was merely an infant spiritually." He twirled the thumbscrews and handed the set to Wilberforce. "Do you know what that is?"

"Yes, Clarkson showed me a set."

"It's a terrible device," said Newton, his eyes on Wilberforce's silver shoe buckles. "But even after my conversion I used them on the slaves! I shudder to think of it. Still, a fact is a fact.

"You see, as I indicated, it takes a long time for God's truths to penetrate our skulls. In time, slavery will be abolished. But as of now, we must have patience, more patience—and still more patience."

"I believe you're right," agreed Wilberforce, his eyes shining. He opened the door and then stopped.

"Yes?" inquired Newton.

"I-I have another problem," confessed Wilberforce. I think I know the answer. Still, your assurance—"

"Speak," said Newton gently. He got up and affectionately put his arm around Wilberforce. "I'm here to help."

"As you know, sir, all who have worked on the Committee are deeply religious people—especially the Quakers. We have worked hard, and we have prayed. And yet we have apparently failed. But over in France where the leaders of the Terror are actually trying to eliminate Christianity, they abolished the Trade and slavery two years ago. And they did it with a mere stroke of a pen. It doesn't seem fair—"

"You mean you wish the French still had slavery?" asked Newton with an impish grin.

"No! Of course not. But—"

"Yes, I know what you mean." A breeze from the lower window fluttered Sunday's sermon notes. Newton settled them with the thumbscrews. "All of us have a common trouble," he said thoughtfully. "We expect God to do everything our way. But God, my friend, is sovereign! A vote in Parliament has no effect on Him. Sometimes—and Christians forget this—He uses non-Christians to do His will. Maybe that's what will happen with the Trade."

"You're probably right," sighed Wilberforce. "But I still can't get those slaves off my mind. Even while we're talking, they're going through a literal hell. I suppose our friend Cowper was right in the hymn we sing, *'God moves in a mysterious way His wonders to perform.'*

"Maybe I should give up and spend my time on some other type of legislation. The poor chimney sweeps need someone to defend them." He squinted at the row upon row of theological books on the shelves by the door. Leaning forward, he said, "My helpers have nearly all given up. I'm standing nearly alone. How can I tell whether or not I should give up? It all seems so hopeless!"

173

"Do you remember our first visit?" asked Newton.

"How could I forget it? You hoisted my sails and adjusted my rudder."

"And didn't I tell you to keep an eye on your spiritual compass?"

"That you did."

"And what does your compass say?"

A lopsided grin crossed Wilberforce's face. "It says, 'You're on the right course. Sail on!' "

"And so, what are you going to do?"

"I'm going to keep my sails high—and sail on."

"What about the fog and the storms?"

"I shall ignore them. Yes, I'll ignore them even when I can't see a hundred feet ahead. I'll keep my eye on the compass and keep sailing until the Trade and slavery itself is completely abolished in the British Empire!" He paused, and then added, "And I hope, John Newton, that you're around when the job is done."

Refreshed, as he always was after a visit with John Newton, Wilberforce returned home. He had started to write a book on Christianity in 1793 and was anxious to complete it. The purpose of the book was to show that Christianity was so vital it should not be confused with mere honor—a popular idea of the eighteenth century.

Although he was still a bachelor, Wilberforce was quite satisfied with his domestic life, even though he was thirty-seven. Marriage, he felt, might hinder his work. Just as the perpetual bachelor, William Pitt, claimed to be married to his country, he felt he was married to one cause—the abolition of slavery.

And then on April 13, a dark-haired, almond-eyed girl named Barbara Spooner changed everything.

16
VICTORY AT LAST!

WILBERFORCE had not been looking for a wife. His concern was abolition. Nevertheless, some of the Claphamites decided that he needed a wife, so Thomas Babington called his attention to Barbara Spooner.

Two days after he first heard of her, Wilberforce and Barbara had dinner together at a party. Nearsighted as he was, he quickly decided that Barbara was a fine girl.

The next day was April 16—Easter Sunday—and he was already having difficulty. He confided to his diary: "Very much affected by my own meditations about Miss Spooner. . . . I'm in danger of falling in love. . . ." On Saturday he wrote: "Supped with the Spooners—captivated with Miss Spooner. . . . My heart gone. . . ."

By April 22 he had proposed! He spent the next day in anxiety. Would she, or would she not accept? Again, he confided in his diary. "This weeks seems a month. Alas—I have seemed too eager about earthly things. It seems as if I have been in a fever. I have constantly, however, prayed to God for His direction and have read His Word."

By the following Tuesday he was in ecstasy. Again he scribbled: "Delightful interview at night for an hour. One of Barbara's hands in mine, the other in her mother's...."

By May 30, the whirlwind romance had ended in marriage. The ecstatic couple managed only a week's honeymoon, and that was spent at one of Hanna Moore's schools at Cowslip Green—a school Wilberforce had been supporting for a number of years.

Back in London, the newly married M.P. plunged again into politics. This was an extremely tense period. Napoleon had won his battles in Italy, and now the little Corsican was threatening to invade England. And to make matters worse, England didn't have a single ally on the continent, and the Channel Fleet at Spithead had mutinied. In addition, the Dutch had become the allies of Napoleon! Bad weather alone had stopped the French from landing in Ireland the previous December.

When Wilberforce tried to talk about abolition during these perilous times, the House laughed him down. "You can't build a new roof in the midst of a hurricane!" scorned an M.P. contemptuously.

Soon Wilberforce had completed his book and titled it *A Practical View of the Prevailing Religious System of Professed Christians in the Higher and Middle Classes in This Country Contrasted with Real Christianity.*

"Will you put your name on the book?" inquired a potential publisher.

"Of course," replied Wilberforce.

"In that case, it might—I say might—sell 500 copies."

Both the publisher and Wilberforce were surprised. The book promptly went through five printings in England, was translated into numerous languages, and was reprinted in America where it enjoyed twenty-five printings. It is still being read.

In 1797 friends of the Trade came up with a clever new ruse. C. R. Ellis, son of a West Indian planter, proposed that because West Indians would be reluctant to accept abolition from Parliament, their own assemblies be encouraged to pass laws which would improve the lot of the slaves. Since such laws would make the slaves happier, they would have more children—and thus the need to import slaves would be eliminated.

It was a smug idea, proposed in a smug way, for a smug purpose.

Wilberforce was incensed. He called the motion an abomination. Later, when he learned that Pitt was willing to back the motion provided there were "modifications," his modest anger flamed into heated fury. Sizzling with dismay, he hurried to the Prime Minister. Pitt listened and was persuaded. "I'll support you to the end," he affirmed.

After the motion was lost, Wilberforce came forward with a new one. Immediately he was denounced by a West Indian planter. This sneering man sarcastically recommended that if Wilberforce wanted to demonstrate his humanity, he should look to his own country where "he would . . . meet a race of blacks as worthy of his benevolent attention as those in the West Indies, namely, the chimney sweeps." Jabbing his finger, he declared that emancipation would cause the slaves to rise in insurrection.

Wilberforce held his breath as the vote was counted. He lost by a margin of 82 to 74. Was he gaining? He persuaded himself to hope so.

While the tug-of-war was going on in the House of Commons, Napoleon, another short man (a mere five feet and one inch), was making Europe his private chessboard. He had remarked, "When I see an empty throne, I feel an urge to sit down on it."

After crowning himself Emperor in Notre Dame Cathedral, Napoleon began to place his friends on all available thrones. His brother, Joseph Bonaparte, became King of Naples; another brother, Louis, King of Holland, and he divided Italy into dukedoms which he bequeathed to favorite generals.

Had it not been for the British fleet, England would have been defeated. This success, however, brought Wilberforce problems. Because of their superiority at sea, the British began to seize French colonies. Would-be planters now demanded fresh supplies of slaves to cultivate their new plantations. This thirst for slaves was increased by the soaring price of sugar. During 1794 sugar brought thirty-two shillings per hundredweight. Four years later it had jumped to eighty-seven shillings per hundredweight.

With plantations cheap—often bought on credit along with a few score of slaves—a man could get rich and retire young.

Again and again Wilberforce attempted to get an abolition bill through the House. Each time he was defeated. Now fresh illnesses and frustrations came upon him like a plague of boils. Sometimes, like Athanasius, he stood alone. Sometimes he felt that his task was like that of a shrimp assigned to devour a whale. And then on February 3, 1801, he suffered a near-fatal blow. William Pitt was forced out of office!

Wilberforce was staggered. True, Pitt had wavered. Still, he could always be counted on by the abolitionists. Wilberforce felt a catch in his throat when he remembered Pitt's famous speech—and especially the end when the early rays of the sun lit up his face and made him seem like a prophet.

Pitt's numerous taxes had cut into his popularity. There was a window tax, a tax on women's headgear (consisting usually of yards of cloth), one on bricks, another on horses, and most hated of all, was the newly created income tax. But the crushing blow, the one that caused him to resign, was when King George refused to allow Irish Catholics to vote.

And now, adding to Pitt's troubles, the King lost his mind again, and blamed it on Pitt! Pitt kept his seat, but he decided that he should work with the soil, and so he bought a farm.

Addington was made the new Prime Minister. Wilberforce liked the man, but he was concerned, for Addington was notoriously cool toward abolition. Studying the situation realistically, Thomas Babington was discouraged. "Why don't you give up?" he asked.

"And let the slaves be thrown to the sharks?" exclaimed Wilberforce.

"But we've tried and failed. God doesn't expect us to do the impossible! You have a fine home, a good wife, and you already have two children. Why don't you retire and write some more books?"

"Don't tempt me, Babington! I've considered doing just what you have suggested for a long time. Still, I can't give up. The Lord put a burden on my soul and I can't shake it off. The slaves must have someone to plead their cause, and I'm going to continue to do so, even if I do look like a shrimp!"

Addington signed the Peace of Amiens with Napoleon. This increased his popularity. Alas, the treaty didn't last and once again Napoleon declared war on England. This was more than Addington could handle, and so Pitt returned to power for the second time as Prime Minister.

And now again war seesawed back and forth on the continent. England had made an alliance with Austria, Sweden, and Russia. Napoleon's ire was up and he determined to smash England, whom he dubbed "the nation of shopkeepers."

Wilberforce was heartbroken. Interest in abolition sank to a new low. Parliament and the man on the street seemed interested in only one thing—war!

Wilberforce prayed that the war would end so that he could get on with abolition. And then he suffered another devastating setback. William Pitt died on January 23, 1806—exactly twenty-five years after he had entered Parliament! He had worked himself to death.

Thinking of his old friend, and the consequences of his death, Wilberforce wept.

Although Fox opposed it, Parliament voted a public funeral for Pitt. He was buried in Westminster Abbey within a few feet of his father. Wilberforce was given the honor of carrying the banner in front of the casket. Speaking to Barbara, he said, "I have three regrets: (1) that Pitt didn't live to see the end of slavery, (2) that he didn't see the end of the war, and (3) that I didn't work hard enough to persuade him to become an evangelical Christian."

"What are the chances for a new abolition bill now?" asked Barbara.

"It all depends on who gets into leadership," replied Wilberforce. "If Addington becomes the Prime Minister there will be no hope at all. Barbara, we must pray that only the right men are elected."

The new government was better than Wilberforce had expected. Lord Grenville became the Prime Minister, Fox headed the Foreign Office, and other abolitionists were given positions of influence.

Mysteriously, there was a personality clash between Grenville and Wilberforce—even though Grenville had been with Pitt the time he asked Wilberforce to undertake the cause of slavery as the three sat under the oak tree at Holwood.

"What do you think of Fox?" asked Barbara one afternoon while they were walking along the Thames.

"I never disliked him as Pitt disliked him," replied Wilberforce, her hand in his. "Fox is a great speaker. But he is also a compulsive gambler—and he always loses. He's lost as much as £30,000 in a single evening. Had his father not been extremely rich, he couldn't have bought his breakfast. His life also is a scandal. When he was accused of arranging the attack on Pitt's carriage, his alibi was that he had been with his mistress! He never goes to church, and as far as I know he has no religion whatever."

Wilberforce paused in front of a slaver anchored in the river. He was silent as he peered through his dim eyes. "But there's one thing about Fox that I admire. He hates slavery. Yes, he hates it with a passion!"

As the happy couple neared their carriage, Wilberforce said, "Barbara, I've asked a special favor of the Lord."

"Yes?"

"I've asked the Lord to abolish the Trade while old John Newton is still alive. But if he's going to grant my request, he'll have to hurry. John is already eighty-two and is getting pretty feeble. A while back, a church officer suggested that he retire. Do you know what Newton said?"

"Tell me."

"His eyes got big and shiny and he swayed back and forth on his tottering legs. Then he all but shouted, 'What! Shall this old African blasphemer stop while he can still speak? Never!'"

Soon Wilberforce began to take courage again. The King regained his senses and Thomas Clarkson enjoyed a new spurt of good health. Indeed, he resumed grinding out abolitionist propaganda as fast as his fingers could write it. A new generation had grown up, and the new generation was convinced that slavery was wrong. The sight of his old friend inspired Wilberforce to predict, "This time, we'll get the bill through!"

On March 31, General Pigott—the attorney who had represented the insurance company in the *Zong* case—presented a bill "to prohibit the importation of slaves in British ships into the colonies annexed by Britain during the war or into the colonies of a foreign state." Like the Dolben bill, it was a compromise to total abolition. However, it represented a softening of the opposition.

The bill zipped through the House of Commons. On its third reading it passed by a vote of 35 to 13. Next, Prime Minister Grenville introduced it into the House of

Lords. There was strong opposition. Nevertheless, it leaped the hurdle of the third reading by a vote of 43 to 13. Wilberforce was so elated, he wrote, "How wonderful are the ways of Providence!"

By the tenth of June, the bill was ready for debate—and Fox was prepared. Although in ill health, he stood before the House and quietly waited for order. Wilberforce watched and prayed. The dropsy that was soon to end his life was clearly evident. His cheeks were swollen, as were his tallowy arms and legs. Soon he began to speak.

"So fully am I impressed," Fox began, "with the importance and necessity of obtaining . . . the object of my motion this day that, if during the almost forty years that I have . . . had the honor of a seat in Parliament, I [am] so fortunate as to accomplish [this] and this only, I . . . [will] have done enough and can . . . retire from public life with . . . the satisfaction that I [did] my duty."

As he spoke, the inverted V formed by his powdered eyebrows was accentuated. Were they announcing a V for victory? Perhaps! As the old opponent of Pitt continued, the fire of his younger days burst into flame and began to crackle and snap. Wilberforce squinted with breathless admiration as he listened.

But the opposition was still there, and soon they began to rehearse their old, old arguments. However, time was against them. When the vote was called, it was 115 for the bill and 15 against the bill.

It also passed in the House of Lords! The abolitionists had gained the second rung of the ladder—the Dolben Bill being the first. Victory was still swirling within the foggy mists—but it was in sight. The abolitionists now had only one theme: total abolition of the Trade!

Again Wilberforce went to work. He was facing his greatest opportunity. From experience he knew that he must not take chances. With this in mind he began to write a burning new tract. He entitled it *A Letter on the Abolition of the Slave Trade*. By the time the sizzling document was finished, it was nearly 400 pages long!

As he waited for the new Parliament to open on December 15, he spent more and more time in prayer. He had a number of anxieties. Would the "tract" be out in time? Would a crisis in the war with Napoleon cause another postponement?

He had hoped that Fox would be able to help him at this critical time. From his sickbed, Fox had expressed an ardent desire to help. Again and again he had said that he longed to go down to the House once more to say something on the Trade. It was not to be. Charles James Fox died during the Parliamentary recess.

Prime Minister Grenville now decided on a startling new strategy. This time the bill would originate in the House of Lords! When he stood in his robes to introduce it on January 2, he was thoroughly prepared—and confident.

The bill was as tough as an oak in Sherwood Forest. It started by declaring that after May 1, 1807, "the African Slave Trade and all manner of dealing and trading in the purchase of slaves in Africa or in their transport to the West Indies or any other island, country, place, or territory whatever is hereby utterly abolished, prohibited, and declared unlawful; and that any of His Majesty's subjects acting to the contrary shall pay £100 for every slave so purchased, sold, or transported."

Opponents immediately went to work. They determined to strangle the bill in the second reading. The tone of their opposition was indicated by Lord Westmorland. With hate-white lips, molded by seething anger, he declared, "Though I should see the Presbyterian and the prelate, the Methodist and the field-preacher, the Jacobin and the murderer unite in support of it in the House, I will raise my voice against it."

Others followed him in a similar way. Still, the bill won by a majority of 68. The next test was the critical third reading.

On February 10, the House of Lords listened to the bill as it was read the third time. Again, it passed. On the same day, the bill was read for the first time in the House of Commons. Many felt that Wilberforce should have had the honor of introducing it. Instead, the bill was read by Lord Howick—the one who had succeeded Fox as Foreign Secretary.

Wilberforce didn't feel slighted. Indeed, he rejoiced, for as a Cabinet member, Howick had more influence than he and thus had a far greater chance to get a majority vote.

After a short debate, supporters of the Trade asked that the second reading be in two weeks rather than the customary one week. Wilberforce winced. He felt it was a trick to give them more time to gather forces and polish their tactics. Nevertheless, Lord Howick granted the request. The next reading was scheduled for February 23.

Wilberforce was nervous. Success had been torn from his hands so often it was hard to believe that it wouldn't happen again. Still, he had hope. He reviewed the list of voters with the Prime Minister. The number of "doubtfuls" was formidable. "I wish I could be certain," sighed Grenville.

Again and again Wilberforce reached into his coat for his New Testament; again and again he closed the door of his closet to be alone with the heavenly Father. At such times the slaves marched into his vision. He could hear the clank of their chains, see their pleading eyes, and hear the sound of splashing as they were tossed to the sharks. Their pitiful groans in the bellies of the slave ships haunted him.

At such times, he prayed through tears, "O Lord, grant my request."

On the crucial morning of February 23, Wilberforce found it difficult to contain his excitement. "This is the day!" he whispered to Barbara, after he had kissed her good-bye. He spent several hours with the Prime Minister and discussed numerous points of strategy. Others, too, were excited—especially the Quakers.

When Wilberforce stepped into the House that evening, he found it was packed. He missed Fox and Pitt. Nevertheless, he knew the Members of Parliament from Clapham were there and that they had been fortified by prayer. Like a watchmaker, Wilberforce was concerned with each detail. A slight technicality could cause delay—perhaps defeat. His book-length tract had been published in time. He wondered if it had had any effect.

The opposition was there, and they were completely prepared. Wilberforce could not see them clearly, but he knew he would soon be hearing them clearly! He prayed that he and his friends would have the right answers. Finally, Lord Howick picked up the bill and began to read it.

Howick was far from being at his best and Wilberforce was concerned. "O Lord, help him," he prayed silently to himself. Perhaps the Foreign Secretary was upset by the tenseness of the House. As he droned on, there was near-silence everywhere. Those who glanced out the three tall windows in the front saw the trees swaying in the wind. Inside, a swarm of lamps flickered and threw shadows across the seats. The galleries were so full many were standing.

The moment Howick finished, six members leaped to their feet. Most were for the bill. Champions of the Trade seemed to know that they had come to their last day. General Gascoyne and Manning spoke against the bill. But their speeches were as ineffective as the curses of a man against a snarling sea.

As the minutes slipped by, the enthusiasm for abolition continued to swell. It was as if a dam had cracked and millions of tons of trapped water were shouldering through and enlarging the crack. This enthusiasm flooded the entire House. It was almost an irresistable force. At the end of each member's speech, he concluded with praises for Wilberforce. This spontaneous adulation reached its climax in the speech given by Sir Samuel Romilly.

The House quieted as Sir Samuel stood. From past experience, everyone knew that he had a reputation for silver-tongued oratory. This evening he was at his best. He compared the selfless projects of Wilberforce to the selfish projects of Napoleon.

At the time there could have been no better comparison, for Napoleon was nearing the summit of his career. He had recently triumphed at Jena and Auerstadt, entered Berlin as a conqueror, and issued an edict which barred British goods from those nations he had subdued.

Said Sir Samuel: "When I look at the man at the head

of the French monarchy, surrounded as he is with the pomp of power and all the pride of victory, distributing kingdoms to his family and principalities to his followers, seeming when he sits upon his throne to have reached the summit of human ambition and the pinnacle of earthly happiness—and when I follow that man into his closet or to his bed, and consider the pangs with which his solitude must be tortured and his repose banished, by the recollection of the blood he has spilled and the oppressions he has committed—"

At this point, the House members appeared to be frozen men, so great was their attention. No one stirred. The most dignified members sat with their mouths slightly ajar.

"And when I compare . . . those pangs of remorse," continued Romilly, "with the feelings which must accompany my honorable friend from this House to his home, after the vote of tonight shall have confirmed the object of his humane and unceasing labors; when he retires . . . to his happy and delighted family, when he lays himself down on his bed, reflecting on the innumerable voices that will be raised in every quarter of the world to bless him, how much more pure and perfect felicity must he enjoy, in the consciousness of having preserved so many millions of his fellow creatures, than—"

At this point, Rommilly was interrupted. Almost the entire membership of the House was on its feet giving Wilberforce a thunderous ovation. Round after round of applause shook the entire building with an intensity greater than any of the present members could remember.

Wilberforce, however, heard little of it. In the midst of

Romilly's eulogy, he had covered his face with his hands and tears streamed down his face and dripped onto his coat.

After the applause had subsided, Mr. Hibbert got to his feet and began to defend the Trade. In his opposition speech, he spoke about the results of a war between two African tribes. He pointed out that slavery had existed before the white man introduced it. "The slaves were each compelled to carry a weight of 100 pounds on their heads for ten miles through mountains, and sometimes twice a day, so that they became bald with the grievous pressure."

The House, however, was tired of such foolish arguments. Soon members began to shout, "Question! Question!"

The decision to abolish the Trade passed by a vote of 283 to 16. It was an overwhelming victory. The rays of a new day were about to emerge over the horizon. Nevertheless, the vote did not mean that the bill had become law. It still faced formidable hurdles. One of these was the committee stage. It survived this on February 27.

After passing this hazard, some jubilant comrades in the fight walked with Wilberforce to his home in Palace Yard. Among these were the Thorntons, the Grants, Granville Sharp, Macaulay, and William Smith.

"What shall we do with those who voted against us?" asked Smith with a chuckle. "I have the names of four!"

Lifting his face from the note he was writing, Wilberforce said, "Never mind the miserable sixteen—let us think of the glorious 283!"

Turning to Henry Thornton, Wilberforce had a playful question. "What shall we abolish next?" he asked.

"The lottery!" said the founder of the Clapham group.

After the group was gone, Wilberforce became unusually serious. "God will bless our country!" he murmured with a positive voice. And then, gathering Barbara into his arms, he added, "Let's keep on praying. Remember victory isn't completely ours until the bill passes the third reading and receives the assent of the King."

"Do you think there is still a chance that we may fail?" asked Barbara after she had snuffed out the candle.

"I sincerely hope not," said Wilberforce yawning. He was tired after a hectic day of excitement.

17
A NEW DAWN

THE BILL to abolish the Trade was presented for its third reading on March 16. There had been objection to the words "justice" and "humanity" in the preamble. With Wilberforce's consent these words were removed. A brief debate followed, with only token resistance.

But now an unexpected thunderhead suddenly appeared. Grenville's government had been tottering for some time. The issue in question was a bill introduced by Grenville to allow Catholics to hold commissions in the army. King George was utterly opposed to the bill, and asked the Prime Minister to promise never to raise the question again. Since Grenville could not agree to this, he resigned in protest.

Thoroughly alarmed, Wilberforce wondered what would happen between governments to the bill abolishing the Trade. But he need not have worried. Perceval, an ardent abolitionist, became the new Prime Minister. Wilberforce breathed a sigh of relief.

The bill went to the House of Lords on March 23, and two days later King George gave his assent. The bill was law!

Wilberforce was overjoyed that John Newton was still alive to witness this triumph, so he hurried over with the good news. "I knew the Lord would answer our prayers!" exclaimed the former slaver as he wiped his eyes. "but now, my son, you have a new task—"

"And what is that?"

"To get a law passed that slavery is completely abolished throughout the entire British Empire. As you know, this law merely ends the Trade—not slavery!"

"Yes, I know. But I have worked for twenty years to get this law through, and I'm already 48!"

"Nonsense! I'm twice as old as you are, and I'm still going strong. Just wait until you hear my sermon on Sunday."

"You're not quite twice as old as I am," laughed Wilberforce.

"Even so, you're still a young man."

"How do you feel?" asked Wilberforce taking both of Newton's hands in his own.

Newton flung an arm around his shoulders. "Listen, young man, I'll tell you how I feel," he replied, his resonant voice amazingly firm. "I feel as if I'm packed and sealed and waiting for the postman!"

William Wilberforce was now a national hero. Regardless of this, because Perceval had dissolved Parliament, he had to stand for reelection. In the 1807 election, he faced two formidable opponents: Milton and Lascelles. Milton ran for the Whigs, Lascelles for the Tories. And since Wilberforce remained an Independent, both men were resolved to crush him. Moreover, their parents put up £200,000 to help them succeed.

"Why don't you withdraw?" suggested the friends of Wilberforce. "You've already accomplished your lifework. Take it easy. Retire."

Wilberforce was tempted to agree. But as Newton had suggested, he knew there was lots of work ahead. Having been busy with abolition, he had not perfected an organization as had the other two. Also, he was not well. Still, he believed he had a chance.

The County of York polls stayed open for fifteen days. At first, it seemed that Milton and Lascelles had outmaneuvered Wilberforce. They had done this, reported the *York Herald*, by hiring nearly all "the barouches, curricles, gigs, flying wagons, and military cars" in and around York for fifteen days! Without transportation, the Wilberforce people could not get to the polls.

But Milton and Lascelles forgot two things, the river and the great respect the people—especially the church people—had for William Wilberforce. Soon the river was crammed with boats on their way to the polls. Also, the farmers lent their wagons and farm animals. Some even rode in on donkeys. Hundreds walked.

By the end of the fourth day, Wilberforce was 111 votes ahead of Milton and 375 ahead of Lascelles. Desperate, his opponents resorted to every sordid trick they could think up. Posters smeared with lies were displayed. Mobsters were employed. And when Wilberforce became ill, they reported him dead.

Still, Wilberforce won. He received 11,806 votes to 11,177 votes for Milton and 10,989 for Lascelles.

With his seat secure, he continued the normal life of a popular politician. He devoted much of his time and resources to philanthropy. Normally, he gave at least 25 percent of his income to others. Sometimes he gave much more.

Wilberforce particularly admired Hannah Moore and her schools. When it came time to forward a donation, he would tear fifty-pound notes in half and mail the sections in separate envelopes. Upon the death of Charles Wesley, he sent his widow a pension for life.

He was often taken in by fakes. Even when he discovered this he merely shrugged. Nothing pleased him more than to pay a man's debts and thus save him from debtor's prison.

Besides letters begging for money, all sorts of people had special requests. Robert Raikes—founder of the Sunday school—begged him to get a position for his son in the West Indies. Pastors wanted him to find them congregations. The brother of Fletcher Christian hoped that he would secure pardons for the mutineers of the *Bounty*. Others wanted him to save criminals from the gallows.

Wilberforce often stayed at his desk until his candles were stumps and his eyes were so dim he could barely see. As old age approached, numerous sorrows crowded into his life. A beloved granddaughter passed away from an unknown disease. In trying to help a son, he invested in a dairy farm, but something went wrong with the deal and he lost £50,000. This did not reduce him to poverty, but it forced him to move into a smaller house and reduce his standard of living.

Another sorrow was that since the Trade was no longer legal, many ships engaged in smuggling slaves to the West Indies and the United States. These blackbirders were heartless men, and a stream of heart-rendering stories came to his ears. For example, there was the grim tale of Captain Homans.

Having sold 5,000 slaves in Cuba, he was not about to give up the Trade because of a miserable law. His brig *Brillante* had a crew of sixty and mounted ten guns. And more than once he fought off ships of the British navy. The time came, however, when he was trapped by four, heavily armed British warships. As they closed in on him at dusk, he knew that he would be boarded the next day, and if his slaves were discovered he would be returned to England in irons.

That night, as the warships waited, he had all 600 of the slaves dragged to the deck and manacled to his heavy anchor chain. At dawn, when he saw his captors approaching he ordered the anchor let down.

The men on the warships heard the slaves scream. But when they boarded the *Brillante* there was not a slave in sight. All that remained were the enormous cooking pots—and the stench. Homan laughed at the gold-braided officers. "Where is the evidence?" he demanded.

When stories like this were related to Wilberforce—and there were many—he shuddered. As he had known all along, the only solution was the total abolition of slavery. But from experience he knew that total abolition would require a long, long fight; and he did not have the health, nor the strength, for such an ordeal. What was he to do? He prayed that God would send a worthy leader to continue the struggle.

In 1817 a thirty-one-year-old by the name of Thomas Fowell Buxton entered the House of Commons as a member from Weymouth. At first his interest was in prison reform and the reduction in crimes to which the death penalty applied. This interest in social reform so interested Wilberforce he began to study the man.

Buxton's father had died when he was only six. He was then brought up by his widowed mother—an ardent Quaker. This Quaker influence was further strengthened when he married the younger sister of Elizabeth Fry Gurney. Elizabeth was an indomitable person. She spearheaded prison reform throughout Europe, raised eleven children, and preached regularly for the Quakers.

Although not a Quaker himself, Buxton was a deeply religious man and a member of the Church of England. About the time he entered Parliament, Samuel Hoare, one of the original committee that had worked with Wilberforce and Clarkson, presented him with a large collection of materials that had been gathered to abolish the Trade.

Buxton studied this material and soon became convinced that all slavery should be abolished.

Letters from the West Indies streamed across Wilberforce's desk. Many of these were from Socrates and missionaries. The letters told how slaves were forced to work from "can to can't time" (dawn to dusk), how they were goaded to work harder by sinister overseers armed with whips, and how they were frequently flogged and even mutilated.

Socrates made drawings of the slaves in the cane fields and of them working in the sugar refineries. Wilberforce replied to all the letters. He made new motions in the House and provided evidence. But now, in addition to his stomach trouble, his lungs became affected. Often he could not appear in the House for days because of the dampness. The fact that he could not do more for the slaves grieved him. And then on May 23, 1821, he heard Buxton address the House on capital punishment. It was a powerful speech.

At the conclusion, he took Buxton to one side. "I would like for you to head the anti-slavery movement," he said.

"I really don't know whether I should do that or not," replied Buxton with great frankness. "I'm all for freeing the slaves, but if we were to free them at this time, it might lead to economic problems—or even revolt."

"But will you agree to pray about it?"

"That, I will, Mr. Wilberforce."

A year and a half later, Buxton was ready. On May 15, 1823, he made a motion in the House of Commons which began: "The state of slavery is repugnant to the principles of the British constitution and Christian religion." He went on to suggest that it should be abolished in steps and "with as much expedition as may be found consistent with a due regard to the well-being of the parties concerned."

Wilberforce supported the motion with a speech.

The West Indies were horrified that such a motion could even be discussed. And when several revolts broke out, their feelings intensified. There was even talk of secession. The opposition to this second crusade was similar to the first one. There were twists and turns, debates, resignations, drastic statements.

During the following year, Wilberforce was stricken with two severe illnesses. One of these was so intense he was unable to do anything for an entire month and had to stay completely out of circulation for the rest of the year.

To a friend, he opened his heart in a letter: "When I consider that my public life is nearly expired, and when I review the many years I have been in it, I am filled with the deepest compunction, from the consciousness of my having made so poor a use of the talents committed to my stewardship. The heart knows its own bitterness. We alone know ourselves, the opportunities we have enjoyed, and the comparative use we have made of them. But it is only to your friendly ear that I breathe out my secret sorrow. I might be supposed by others to be fishing for a compliment. Well, it is an unspeakable consolation that we serve a gracious Master who giveth liberally and upbraideth not."

Sir John Sinclair sympathized with Wilberforce's dilemma, and he proposed a solution. It could be arranged for Wilberforce to be made a peer. This would put him in the House of Lords for life. His duties would be lighter in the Upper House and he would never have to campaign for election.

Friends considered this a splendid opportunity and urged him to accept. Wilberforce declined. He feared acceptance would make it appear that he had sought honors and would thus reflect on his Christianity. Also a peerage would make his children part of the nobility, and he feared this would cause their Christian lives to suffer.

After forty-five years in the House of Commons, Wilberforce retired on February 1, 1825. In his retirement he was often asked to appear on platforms and make speeches. Such appearances always drew large crowds. But as he aged, he began to tire easily.

The old fighter of slavery had always been a dreamer

and one to reflect on the past. Every November 15 he remembered Pitt's birthday. In 1827, he wrote: "Poor Pitt dead above twenty-one years; today he would have been sixty-eight." When friends discussed the former Prime Minister, Wilberforce always said, "I never knew such an extraordinary man."

During these years, he indulged in a nostalgic trip to the places of his youth. Alas, it was not the joyful trip he had hoped. Old landmarks had been moved, and often when he inquired about a friend, he would be told, "Oh, he's been dead for many years now."

Wilberforce still retained his gift of conversation—and mimicry. Often at a family gathering, he would be urged to mimic a public figure. On these occasions, his performance would be so accurate the group would howl with laughter. Then, conscience-smitten, he always added a few kind words about his victim.

During these years he hoped to write a book on the New Testament epistles, but it seemed that he could never get started.

In April 1833, during his seventy-third year, Wilberforce was asked to make a motion against slavery at the town hall in Maidstone. In recent years he had refused all such invitations. But since this speech was to be a motion against slavery, he accepted with enthusiasm.

On the twelfth, he gingerly stepped onto the platform and made what was to be his last public appearance. Wilberforce felt that when the slaves were freed, their owners should be compensated by the British government. He boldly declared, "I say, and I say honestly and fearlessly, that the same Being who commands us to love mercy, says also, 'do justice'; and therefore I have no objection to grant the colonists the relief that may be due to them."

His voice was quite feeble and failed to fill the hall as it had filled the much smaller House of Commons. The audience had to strain to hear.

Toward the end of the speech, Wilberforce said, "I trust that we now approach the end of our career—." He had just said this when a shaft of light came through the window and illuminated his face just as a similar one had illuminated the face of William Pitt forty-one years before. Inspired by this amazing coincidence, he exclaimed with new vigor, "The object is bright before us, the light of heaven beams on it and is an earnest of success."

Sometime later Wilberforce was seen sitting at the dinner table. He was weary, his eyes were lackluster, and he seemed totally unconcerned about what was going on. Then someone mentioned that the new debates on slavery were about to commence in the House of Commons. This news completely transformed him. Leaping from his chair, he drew himself to his full height, and facing his guests as if he were facing a packed House, he cried with great clarity, "Hear! Hear!" It was a spine-tingling incident.

Three months later Wilberforce was so ill with his old stomach trouble and other complications he was moved to a house in Cadogan Place—about a mile from the House of Commons. When asked how he felt, he replied with a wry smile, "I am like a clock that is almost run down."

Among his visitors was a youth by the name of William Gladstone—who would later distinguish himself as a Christian statesman and Prime Minister during the reign of Queen Victoria. Gladstone mentioned the occasion in his diary: "He is cheerful and serene, a beautiful picture of old age in sight of immortality. Heard him pray with his family. Blessings and honor are on his head."

As Wilberforce wrestled with approaching death, Stanley's bill for total abolition was being debated in the House of Commons. The West Indies were thoroughly alarmed. Their prosperity—so they claimed—had tipped the balances against Napoleon. And now they wailed that freeing their slaves would ruin them. As late as May 1833, Elizabeth Barrett—afterward the wife of Robert Browning—wrote to a friend, "The West Indies are irreparably ruined if the Bill passes. Papa says that in the case of its passing, nobody in his senses would think of even attempting the cultivation of sugar, and that they had better hang weights to the sides of the island of Jamaica and sink it at once."

Elizabeth, however, retained a warm feeling toward the slaves. After the legislation was passed, she wrote in another letter: "Of course you know the Bill has ruined the West Indians. . . . The consternation here is very great. Nevertheless, I am glad, and always shall be, that the Negroes are virtually free."

The prospective bill was revised several times. In the final version a gift of twenty million pounds was to be made to the masters. This part of the legislation was approved on July 24 by the margin of 158 votes to 151.

A reduction in the length of the apprenticeship was agreed to the next day, and this time there was no opposition.

July 26, 1833, was Friday. As the bill came up for the second reading, the abolitionists were worried. But since the government was sponsoring the bill, Wilberforce was confident. Assured of its passage during the debates, Lord Stanley—remembering the tireless efforts of the dying man from Hull—remarked, "When Mr. Wilberforce hears it, he may well exclaim, 'Lord, now lettest Thou Thy servant depart in peace.'"

The second reading of the bill passed without difficulty. Upon learning of the twenty million pounds of compensation,° Wilberforce expressed his satisfaction by exclaiming, "Thank God that I should have lived to witness a day in which England is willing to give twenty million sterling for the abolition of slavery."

Shortly after the bill survived the second reading, a visitor at the place where Wilberforce was staying, said, "I don't think he can last long." In spite of this prediction, the old slave fighter survived the night and led the family and servants in morning worship. Afterward, as an aged servant wheeled him through the garden, Wilberforce seemed unusually animated and visited at length with his beloved employee.

The passage of the bill had been a tonic!

By Sunday, Wilberforce was much worse. That evening in a moment of consciousness, he muttered, "I am in a very distressed state."

"Yes," replied his son Henry, "but you have your feet on the Rock."

"I do not venture to speak so positively," replied Wilberforce, "but I hope I have." Those were his last words. At three o'clock on Monday morning, he gave one last sigh and was gone. Had he lived another month, he would have been seventy-four.

°Robin Furneaux estimates that this was about one half of the market value of the slaves.

Almost immediately upon the news of his passing, the authorities in Parliament requested that his body be laid to rest in Westminster Abbey. Permission was granted by the family. Both Houses of Parliament were recessed on the day of the funeral—August 5.

As the time for the services neared, a long line of carriages began to form between Cadogan Place and the Abbey. Immense crowds flanked the line of carriages in moving columns on either side.

Among the pallbearers were the Speaker of the House, the Lord Chancellor, and the Duke of Gloucester. The body was laid to rest at a favorite spot near the remains of Pitt and Fox. Writing to the sons of Wilberforce, a friend noted: "You would like to know that as I came towards [the Abbey] down the Strand, every third person I met going about their ordinary business was in mourning."

Nearly a year later, at midnight, July 31, 1834, approximately 800,000 slaves were declared free.° The fight in Parliament had lasted nearly half a century, but the accomplishment was surely worth all the effort. The man who resembled a shrimp and who was handicapped by poor health most of his life had shown the world that a righteous cause, coupled with determination and motivated by faith in a loving God, can produce miracles.

When the news of his death reached the West Indies, many slaves went into mourning—as did the free blacks in the United States.

°Although technically freed on this date, the slaves were required to continue working for their masters in what was termed an apprenticeship. The length of the apprenticeship ranged from six years for field laborers to four years for artisans. During this period the masters were required to feed, clothe, and house them. They were also required to pay wages for all work over forty-five hours a week.

In 1836 a team of Quakers—including Joseph Sturge, Thomas Harvey, John Scoble, and William Lloyd—went to the West Indies to see how the apprenticeship system was working. In Antigua, Sturge was told by the local planters that they were making better profits with paid labor than they had with slaves.

The Quakers were not displeased with what they saw, except that they were annoyed at the excessive punishment which was frequently meted out to the slaves.

During this period many planters decided that without slaves they would have to improve their methods. These new methods increased profits. Inspired by what could happen, the Quakers made many sensible suggestions. Largely due to their efforts, on their return home, apprenticeship was terminated on August 1, 1838, the day celebrated in the West Indies as Emancipation Day. In the end the planters welcomed the discontinuance of apprenticeship as much as their slaves.

About a year after his passing, a marble statue of Wilberforce was placed in the Abbey. The long epitaph, perhaps written by Lord Thomas Babington Macaulay, concludes:

> Here to Repose:
> Till, through the Merits of Jesus Christ,
> His only Redeemer and Savior,
> (Whom, in His Life and in His Writings He Had Desired to Glorify)
> He shall Rise in the Resurrection of the Just.

BIBLIOGRAPHY

The basic source for all biographies of William Wilberforce go back to the five-volume set issued by his sons, Robert Isaac and Samuel Wilberforce. The largest collection of Wilberforce documents in the United States is in the William R. Perkins Library at Duke University.

In addition to the above sources, the author has made use of the following (of these, by far the most important has been the excellent volume, *William Wilberforce* by Robin Furneaux, issued by Hamish Hamilton, Ltd., and copyrighted by Robin Furneaux in 1974):

Aykroyd, W. R. *Sweet Malefactor*. William Heinemann, Ltd., 1967.

Barnes, Donald Grove. *George III and William Pitt—1783-1806*. Stanford, Calif.: Stanford University Press, 1939.

Besant, Sir Walter. *London in the Eighteenth Century*. London, 1925.

——————————. *London in the Nineteenth Century*. London, 1910.

Burns, W. L. *Emancipation and Apprenticeship in the West Indies*. Jonathan Cape, London, 1937.

Churchill, Sir Winston. *A History of the English-Speaking People, Vol. III*. New York: Dodd and Mead, 1957.

Clarkson Thomas. *History of the Abolition of the Slave Trade, Vols. I and II*. Frank Cass, Ltd., London.

Copeland, Thomas W. *Our Eminent Friend, Edmund Burke*. New Haven: Yale Press, 1949.

Coupland, R. *A Narrative*. Oxford, 1923.

Dawsons of Pall Mall. *Slave Trade Debates.* London, 1806.
Dow, George Francis. *Slaves, Ships, and Slaving.* Marine Research Society, 1927.
Derry, John W. *Charles James Fox.* New York: St. Martin's Press, 1972.
Ehrman, John. *The Younger Pitt.* New York: E. P. Dutton, 1969.
Ekwall, Eilert. *Street Names of the City of London.* Oxford, 1954.
Eyck, Erich. *Pitt Versus Fox, Father & Son.* G. Bell and Sons, Ltd., London, 1950.
Furneaux, Robin. *William Wilberforce.* Hamish Hamilton, 1974.
Grieve-Mackenzie, Averil. *The Last Years of the English Slave Trade.* Frank Cass and Co., Ltd., London.
Hamshere, Cyril. *The British in the Caribbean.* Cambridge: Harvard University Press, 1972.
Jarrett, Derek. *Pitt the Younger.* New York: Scribners, 1974.
Lowenthal, David. *Slaves, Free Men, Citizens.* Anchor Books, 1973.
Marshall, Dorothy. *The English Poor in the Eighteenth Century.* Routledge & Kegan Paul, Ltd.
Mathieson, William Law. *British Slave Emancipation, 1838-1849.* New York: Octagon Books, 1967.
Pares, Richard. *A West Indian Fortune.* Archon Books, 1968.
Porter, Dale H. *The Abolition of the Slave Trade in England.* Archon Books, 1970.
Shyllon, F. O. *Black Slaves in Britain.* Oxford University Press, Institute of Race Relations, 1974.
Trevelyan, G. M. *Illustrated English Social History.* New York: David McKay, 1942.
Underhill, Edward Bean. *The West Indies.* Westport, Conn.: Negro University Press.
Wedgewood, Josiah. *The Selected Letters of Josiah Wedgwood.* Josiah Wedgwood and Sons, Ltd.
Warner, Oliver. *William Wilberforce.* Arco Publishing Co., 1962.

CHARLES LUDWIG, a free-lance writer since 1940, lives with his wife, Mary (Puchek), in Tucson, Arizona.

Ludwig has pastored five congregations, has preached throughout Western Europe, and has conducted more than 300 evangelistic campaigns.

He attended Indiana State Teacher's College, Boise Junior College, and received his BS from Anderson College. Gulf Coast College awarded him a DD degree in 1973.

More than 1,200 articles by Charles Ludwig have appeared in nearly 100 magazines. His 35 books carry the imprint of many publishers, both in the United States and abroad.

While in Kenya at the age of ten he met his first freed slave. This was Matthew Wellington, David Livingstone's last surviving porter.

The Ludwigs have two children—both of them high school teachers.